Montana State Irrigation Convention

Report of Proceedings of the second State Irrigation Convention

Held at Helena, Montana, February 9 and 10, 1893

Montana State Irrigation Convention

Report of Proceedings of the second State Irrigation Convention
Held at Helena, Montana, February 9 and 10, 1893

ISBN/EAN: 9783337185596

Printed in Europe, USA, Canada, Australia, Japan

Cover: Foto ©ninafisch / pixelio.de

More available books at **www.hansebooks.com**

REPORT OF PROCEEDINGS

OF THE

SECOND

State . Irrigation . Convention

HELD AT

HELENA, MONTANA,

February 9 and 10, 1893.

With Reports of the State of Irrigation in Several
Counties.

GREAT FALLS, MONT.
PRESS OF THE LEADER COMPANY.
1893.

SECOND ANNUAL SESSION

OF THE

STATE ❀ IRRIGATION ❀ CONVENTION.

The State Irrigation Convention was called to order Thursday, February 9, 1893, at 11 o'clock a. m., in the Board of Trade rooms, Helena, by H. P. Rolfe, of Great Falls, chairman of the executive committee appointed by the first irrigation convention in January, 1892.

Mayor Curtin of Helena welcomed the delegates in the following address:

Gentlemen of the Irrigation Convention: This convention is opportune. I congratulate you upon the time, place and purpose of your meeting. No subject is engaging the public mind more and none deserves more consideration and thorough attention than the question of irrigation. Every man of experience or observation in this state appreciates the great possibilities that await a well directed and comprehensive system of irrigation. Various and divergent views are presented as to the manner of accomplishing the most beneficial results. Should the state, under the constitutional provision declaring the use of water to be "a public use," assume to regulate and control that use, or shall the whole matter be left to individual or corporate control?

Your convention is composed of gentlemen possessing a wide range of learning, supplemented by close observation and experience of all that relates to a proper solution of the questions submitted to your consideration and discussion, and I have no doubt that the conclusions you reach will go far toward molding sentiment and shaping legislation in the right direction.

You will find that quite a number of the citizens of Helena have been active and earnest in pressing the irrigation question on the attention of the people, conscious that a speedy and proper solution of it will result in great and permanent prosperity to the whole state.

Omitting any observations at this time as to the proper methods to be adopted or recommended, and assuring you that no community in the state feels a livelier interest in the result of your deliberations, I extend you a most cordial welcome to Helena.

Gov. Rickards sent a letter expressing his regret at his inability to be present. Letters were read by the secretary, S. B. Robbins, from the general passenger agents of the Northern Pacific and Great Northern railroads in reference to transportation.

The following committee on credentials was appointed: Z. T. Burton, Choteau; J. A. Brown, Beaverhead; C. H. Hardenbrook, Deer Lodge; S. Deutsch, Park county, and W. H. Sutherlin, Meagher county.

The following committee on permanent organization, consisting of one member from each county represented, was appointed: W. M. Oliver, Beaverhead; W. D. Cooper, Choteau; G. Sheets, Custer; W. F. Parker, Cascade; Charles Mussigbrod, Deer Lodge; J. M. Robinson, Gallatin; A. H. Nelson, Lewis and Clarke; J. E. Kanouse, Meagher; P. Carney, Madison; I. D. O'Donnell, Yellowstone; E. Ryan, Jefferson; W. F. Shanks, Park.

After which a recess was ordered until 2 p. m. to await the reports of the committees.

THURSDAY AFTERNOON.

At 2 p. m. the convention was called to order by Chairman Rolfe.

The committee on credentials reported as follows: That the following delegates were present and entitled to seats in the convention:

Beaverhead—W. R. Gilbert, James Edie, Charles Padley, W. M. Oliver, J. E. Morse, B. F. White, R. C. Halliday, J. A. Brown, W. T. Maulden, Phil. Lovell.

Cascade—S. B. Robbins, W. F. Parker, N. T. Porter, H. P. Rolfe, C. H. Wright, J. O. Gregg, M. S. Burns, J. Bookwalter, D. J. Tallant, D. W. Beecher.

Choteau   J. W. Power, U. G. Allen, Charles Blackman, Thomas O'Hanlon, Milt Cooper, Julius Hirshberg, E. E. Leech, T. C. Burns, W H. Green, Z. T. Burton.

Custer—W. N. Haynes, L. A. Huffman, Geo. Schutz, J. R. McKay.

Gallatin—John M. Robinson, Charles Sales, George Kinkle, Jr. W. W. Alderson, B. F. Shuart, Chas. P. Blakely, Thomas Reece. A. K. Stanton, J. A. Luce, Arthur Truman.

Deer Lodge—D. M. Durfee, Andrew Whitesides, G. W. Morse, John Blair, N. J. Bielenberg, Israel Gibbs, John Goff, Charles Mussigbrod, J. E. Hyde, C. K. Hardenbrook, W. L. Hoye.

Jefferson—Ed. Ryan, A. C. Quaintance, A. Belcher, Jesse Patterson, R. W. Noble, C. W. Brooke, A. Macomber, W. U. Williams, Henry Reed, John Keating.   Alternates—Wm. Kennedy, T. J. Galbraith, S. C. Harris.

Lewis and Clarke—S. T. Hauser, T. H. Carter, W. C. Child, E. D. Weed, D. A. Cory, H. M. Parchen, C. K. Wells, T. E. Crutcher, A. H. Nelson, G. C. Swallow.   Alternates—A. M. Holter, Peter Winne, Donald Bradford, W. M. G. Settles, Norman Holter, W. A. Haven, Sen. W. F. Sanders.

Madison—Hon. S. R. Buford, Patrick Carney, J. B. Jeffers; Alex. Metzel, John T. Connor, R. O. Hickman, W. A. Gray

Meagher—J. E. Kanouse, D. E. Folsom, Wm. Sutherlin, J. A. Woodson, W. E. Tierney, N. E. Benson, H. S. Hyatt, Wm. Mueller, Ed. Cooney, G. V. Stafford.

Missoula—G. W. Ward, L. C. Loring, Fred Whiteside, Frank Higgins, Thos. C. Marshall, Chas. M. Crutchfield.

Park—S. Deutsch, Thos. P. McDonald, Alfred Myers, J. M. Conrow, W. Shanks, H. J. Hoppe.

Silver Bow—John Caplice, Lee Mantle, Geo. Irvine II.

Yellowstone—Fred H. Foster, I. D. O'Donnell, Fred Sweetman, Chas. J. Spear, Frank Whitney, J. R. Goss, John Ramsey, A. Graham, Paul McCormick.

The report was adopted, and the committee was continued to report further as the delegates arrived.

The committee on permanent organization, through its chairman, W. M. Oliver, reported the following names for permanent officers:

President—H. P. Rolfe, Cascade.

Secretary—S. B. Robbins, Cascade.

Treasurer—W. H. Sutherlin, Meagher.

Vice Presidents—R. O. Hickman, Madison; C. Hardenbrook,

Deer Lodge; Alfred Myers, Park; A. M. Holter, Lewis and Clarke.

The committee also reported the following order of business:

Thursday Afternoon Appointment of committee on irrigation laws, to consist of one from each county; appointment of committee to give reports on irrigation in each county in the state, represented in this meeting; appointment of committee on constitution and by-laws; reading of papers; discussion of best methods of building irrigation canals and reservoirs; adjournment.

Evening Session, at 7:30 -Address by Lieut.-Gov. Botkin; discussion of the irrigation law now before the legislature.

Friday, 10 a. m.- -Report of county committees; report of committee on irrigation law. Afternoon—Report of committee on constitution and by-laws: election of permanent officers for ensuing year; memorials to congress, and miscellaneous subjects.

On motion the officers named in the report were duly elected, and the order of business as read was adopted.

The president, H. P. Rolfe, having thanked the convention for the honor, took his seat, and announced as the first order of business the appointment of the committee on irrigation law, and asked for names to be suggested from each county. The following members were appointed:

A. H. Nelson, chairman, Lewis and Clarke; W. R. Gilbert, Beaverhead; W. F. Parker, Cascade; Z. T. Burton, Choteau; L. A. Hoffman, Custer; D. M. Durfee, Deer Lodge; A. C. Quaintance, Jefferson; J. M. Robinson, Gallatin; W. H. Sutherlin, Meagher; G. W. Ward, Missoula; A. B. Myers, Park; I. D. O'Donnell, Yellowstone; P. Carney, Madison.

The next business in order being that of the appointment of a committee on constitution and by-laws, the following were appointed:

Z. T. Burton, chairman, Choteau; C. H. Wright, Cascade; B. F. Shuart, Gallatin; G. C. Swallow, Lewis and Clarke; John T. Connor, Madison.

Prof. Swallow then made a motion that a committee of five engineers be appointed to make a report on the subject of the construction of canals and reservoirs. Referred to committee on constitution and by-laws.

On motion a committee was appointed to give reports from each county on the status of irrigation, as follows:

Jos. A. Browne, Beaverhead; N. T. Porter, Cascade; U. G. Allen, Choteau; J. R. McKay, Custer; Chas. Mussigbrod, Deer Lodge; Ed. Ryan, Jefferson; W. W. Alderson, Gallatin; Donald Bradford, Lewis and Clarke; J. E Kanouse, Meagher; G. W. Ward, Missoula;

T. B. McDonald, Park; I. D. O'Donnell, Yellowstone; R. O. Hickman, Madison.

It was moved by Mr. Nelson that the convention invite the state legislature to be present at session this evening. The motion was carried, and Messrs. Nelson and Burton were selected as messengers to transmit the invitations.

A recess was then taken to allow committee on constitution and by-laws to report at this session. The committee on by-laws and constitution stated that they could not report till tomorrow and were given further time.

After some preliminary discussion on the subject of irrigation generally and the reading of a paper on the subject by John M. Robinson of Gallatin, the roll of counties was called for reports on the state of irrigation in each. I. D. O'Donnell of Yellowstone said there was lots of water in his section, but what they wanted now principally was more ditches, and the farmers would like to own the big ones. Crops had been very successful in the past season. The ceded portion of the Crow reservation recently thrown open to settlement afforded an excellent opportunity for the small farmers who would raise chickens, fruits, hogs and such products. Helena, Butte and other towns which now import their articles of consumption by the thousands of tons would give the small holder of land a ready market for the products of his farm. Dr. G. C. Swallow said that was just what Montana needed, men who would be content with 160 acres; we don't want the big farmers. Fred Whiteside of Missoula echoed these views, but said the water for irrigation must first be provided, and then it would be time enough to invite the small farmer to cultivate the land.

Some startling facts were brought to light by C. H. Wright of Cascade as to the amount of money paid out by the people of that county for food brought into the state that Mr. Wright said should be produced here. Mr. Wright then read the report of the special committee of the board of trade of the city of Great Falls, prepared by Mr. W. M. Bole, of the Leader, as follows:

To the Chairman of the Board of Trade:

SIR—In pursuance to a resolution of the Board of Trade appointing me on a committee to ascertain, with such exactness as might be possible, the amount of money which is annually sent out of this city and county in payment for farm products such as might have been produced within the limits of this county, I beg leave to report that I have made as thorough an investigation into the matter as my time and sources of information would permit, and I find that the gross value of such imported products of the farm amounts to the sum of $366,572, divided as follows.

Smoked meats.......$127,522 34	Potatoes ....$ 3,000 00
Flour 51,434 00	Butter 44,000 00
Pork.............. 45,600 00	Cheese.............. 5,364 00
Eggs.............. 42,400 00	Oatmeal 6,152 00
Poultry 19,700 00	Cornmeal 5,300 00
Apples 6,300 00	Vegetables, fruits..... 9,800 00

Total...$366,572 34

The value of any statistics, and especially such statistics as
these, depends of course on their completeness and accuracy, and I
deem it proper and just that I should supplement this report by a
few remarks in regard to the manner in which they were obtained
and the reliability and completeness of the various items. Smoked
meats is an item which heads the list and which is supplied almost
entirely from outside the state, taking out of the pockets of the people of Cascade county the enormous sum of $127,522.34, according to
the returns received from the merchants of the county. One firm
alone pays out over $40,000 per annum for this commodity, and an-
other firm follows close on these figures.

The next heaviest item on the list is flour, which amounts to
$51,434 per annum. Little need be said on this topic, as it will un-
doubtedly dwindle to insignificant proportions or disappear altogether within the next year, when our new flouring mill gets into operation.

Pork and lard comes next on the list, costing $45,600, and of
course all that has been said on the subject of smoked meats applies
equally to this topic. I am assured that all the pork raised in this
county in a year would not supply the market in this city a week
and that a good high figure is always obtainable here for home-
raised pork.

Eggs, butter and poultry are three items which have always
been able to meet with a ready sale here and considerable quantities
are brought in from the surrounding country and sold here by the
farmers, and yet there has been over $100,000 sent out of the country
to make up the deficit between the supply and demand. I am told
by a large dealer in butter that a better price could be obtained by
the local farmers for this product if a creamery was established here
as the demand is for a better keeping butter than the dairy butter
usually is. The item of potatoes, which is put down at $3,000,
is one which in some years amounts to a large sum. The $3,000
charged to this item was for shipments made within a few weeks.
Up to this time sufficient potatoes could be obtained at home, but
the supply is now said to be about exhausted and a considerable
quantity will have to be shipped in before the new crop becomes
available. Apples are another item in the list amounting to $6,300,
which I believe to be below the actual figures. That they can be
successfully raised here is maintained by some who have given the
subject attention. Oatmeal, cornmeal and vegetables aggregate
about $20,000 more.

As I said before, statistics such as these are only valuable as
they are accurate, and a few words will be in place as to how they
were obtained. A blank form was left with every wholesale and retail merchant in town, containing a list of the various farm products

in question, and a request made of them that they fill up the form with a statement of the amount of each item imported by them from abroad during the year. These were afterward gathered and collated as given above.

There is a class of importers of farm products of which no account has been made in these figures, and that is the small hotels, boarding houses and private families.

Taking these various items into account, I believe it to be a moderate estimate to say that the total amount of money which goes out of Cascade county in one year for the purchase of the farm products above mentioned will come very close to $500,000. The effect of keeping in the pockets of the people of the county this vast sum of money, or even half of it, is something too obvious to be dilated on. It would mean new life blood circulating through all the veins and arteries of trade and commerce in this section of the state.

Major Alderson of the Gallatin county delegation said the trouble with the Gallatin county farmers was that they could not always dispose of all their produce. There was a prejudice against flour made there, although enough was turned out by the mill to feed half of the population of Montana. The mills had tried to sell their flour in Helena and Butte but with indifferent success, especially in the capital city. The millers, however, got around this difficulty by placing the Montana flour in Minnesota sacks, and no one complained. All the eggs, bacon and chickens raised in the Gallatin valley are consumed there. The only thing they exported was the barley, which has been pronounced to be superior to any raised in the United States.

J. M. Robinson gave prices of products of Gallatin county.

Peter Winne of Helena told the delegates about his experience in Colorado, a state which had gone all through what Montana is now dealing with. He had seen Denver grow from a small place until it reached a population with a pay roll of 11,000 mechanics. All the difficulties had been overcome by patience, and so it will be with Montana. Referring to the prejudice against Montana flour, he said he thought perhaps it was not made right. He had sampled some himself which was not very good.

B. F. Shuart of Gallatin did not think there was any necessity for bringing any more farmers into Montana. The times had changed, and now there was overproduction. Colorado and other states were sending into this state their overproduction, a serious thing for the Montana farmer. People who lived in cities were always trying to tell the farmers how to carry on their business. The idea of bringing in small farmers to raise chickens was all very well, but his experience had been that it was not always convenient for every farmer to carry out the fads proposed by the city people.

What the state needed now was more bread consumers rather than more producers.

An entirely opposite view and one which seemed to meet the approval of the convention was advanced by I. D. O'Donnell of Yellowstone. He took a very hopeful view of the future and said the present was full of promise. He told of men who came to the Yellowstone country five years ago without money and who are now the owners of good improved farms and worth $5,000 to $10,000. As an instance of the soil, he told of one who raised $2,400 worth of fruit last year. They were all doing well and seemed to be more in touch with the times than the almanac farmer. Most of them were satisfied with small holdings, and all of them would do well. He didn't think there was anything wrong with the Montana farmer who attended to his business. There were some of them who had become so successful that they had moved into town and built fine residences and there were others who spent their winters in California.

It was then moved to have a stenographer take down the future proceedings of the convention. The motion was carried. A recess was then taken till evening.

THURSDAY EVENING.

At 8 p. m. President Rolfe called the convention to order, and announced the first exercise of the evening to be the address of Lieut.-Gov. Botkin.

Gov. Botkin then delivered the following address upon the Chemistry of Irrigation:

The people of the United States are in the habit of boasting that ours is the greatest agricultural country on the globe. In some respects this is true. It is true as regards the variety of our products, but that follows from the fact that our area embraces every kind of climate, from antarctic to tropical. It is probably true as to acreage, but this again is only to say that we have a domain so vast that it stretches from perpetual snow to perpetual summer, and that as the last rays of the setting sun gild the tops of our Alaskan peaks, the light of the coming morning flashes upon the rocks of Maine. It is true of the number and variety of the mechanical appliances which we employ and which we have contributed to the agriculture of the world. If there is any labor-saving device in common use in the cultivation of the soil that is not an American invention, I never happened to hear of it.

But it is conspicuously untrue of the methods which we practice so far as regards developing the largest possibilities of production in a given tract of land. Here we might with profit seek elementary instruction from the Japanese, whom we are in the habit of looking upon as a people the reverse of progressive. They have not failed to meet the necessities arising from the ratio of their population to their tillable area. Their agriculture is based upon the fundamental principle that the sole duty of the soil is to afford mechanical support to the plant and to act as the reservoir and conduit of its food. The duty of feeding it is quite another matter, and that devolves upon the farmer. He would no more neglect to feed the growing vegetable than we would neglect to feed a pig or calf that we would rear to usefulness, and it cannot be doubted that is the true theory of agriculture.

I learned recently of a change that has come over the farming industry of my native state of Wisconsin. Its rich loam with a subsoil of clay seemed to be inexhaustible in its fertility, but of course it was not without its limitations. Intelligent farmers engaged largely in raising blooded stock and delivered the products of their land on their legs to a hungry market, and so, it may be said, got there with four feet. They soon were able to buy out their thriftless neighbors, who, it is to be apprehended, thereupon moved farther west, principally to the Dakotas. Then came another change. The owners of large farms in Wisconsin, and presumably in the neighboring states, found it to advantage to let them in small holdings to immigrants from the agricultural countries of Europe, who have been taught to make the utmost possible use of every square foot of ground. They themselves removed to the adjacent cities, where they would enjoy greater social and educational advantages. These changes involve a new system of landlordism and threaten a recurrence to feudal conditions which have a political aspect that is far from hopeful. The consideration of this would be wholly alien to my subject; but it may be confidently stated that it would be a sad day for the republic when it should become a rule and not the exception that the cultivation of the soil is separated from its ownership. The possession by the citizen of the land that he tills is one of the strongest muniments of our institutions.

The processes by which irrigation nourishes growing crops—behold my theme! Many years ago, an interesting experiment was tried. Common sand was first thoroughly cleansed by boiling in nitro-muriatic acid, which was then carefully removed by washing in water. Next, seeds of various grains were deposited in the sand and moisture supplied. Barley and oats sprouted and grew to the height of eighteen inches; they blossomed but did not come to seed, and soon withered, drooped and died. The same results followed when, instead of sand, a mass of horsehair was used to sustain the plant and consume the moisture. It may be stated particularly that there is something wanting in the report of these experiments, as it does not appear that the water used was first distilled. If not, it may be surmised that it provided in part the ingredients that insured the growth of the stock. That, however, permits of another explanation in the gluten, stalk and other substances that are furnished by the seed itself.

Then the experiment was varied. To the sand were added certain mineral acids prepared in the laboratory. Seeds of the same plants were deposited in the artificial soil so prepared, and they grew luxuriantly. Barley, oats and other grains sent up strong stalks, blossomed, and yielded ripe and perfect seeds. The difference in the first and second experiment illustrates completely the difference between negligent farming in exhausted soils and scientific agriculture.

It has been mentioned that the seed itself supplies some of the ingredients of nutrition, but necessarily in a very limited quantity. The germinal principle in a grain of wheat, for example, constitutes only a minute part of its contents. The rest consists of starch, gluten and certain mineral substances, and so the young plant, like the young animal, in the first stages of its growth is fed by its mother. The nutriment that is thus provided is just sufficient to sustain it until its organs are so far developed as to enable it to procure its own food. It sends its roots downward, extends its tender stalk upward, throws out its delicate leaflets, and thereafter must derive its sustenance from the earth and air.

The latter process is not within the limits of our subject. Carbon, which in quantity is the most important constituent of the plant, is largely derived from the atmosphere. The tiny leaflets absorb carbonic acid, decompose it, retain the carbon and surrender the oxygen. The water or sap conveyed through the infinitesimal capillaries of the plant acts upon the carbon, and the two build the cellulose tissue that constitutes the stalk. In the meantime the plant is sending its roots into the earth in search of the other food that is necessary to its growth, in other words, if our longitude will furnish an excuse for its expression, "rustling for grub."

This brings us to the office of irrigation in the cultivation of crops. The necessity of water commences with the first beginning of growth and continues without ceasing to the full maturity of the seeds. The seed must be thoroughly saturated before germination can commence. Then during the period when the young plant is obliged to live upon the store of nutrients contained in the seed, it is water that conveys them to the newly developed parts. This function is continued after the plant begins to draw its supply of nitrogen compounds and mineral substances from the soil, a process which, as we shall see, depends in other respects upon the assistance of water. The proportion of water in all vegetables is very large, from 80 per cent. in most cereals to 96 per cent. in turnips. Within the period of active growth of a stalk of wheat or barley, it requires the passage through it of not less than a gallon of water. The earth is not profligate with its store of moisture; it gives it up to the plant rather grudgingly, and when it is reduced to less than 10 per cent. it withholds it altogether. Hence the adjacent ground must be kept supplied with water, or the growth of the crop will be wholly arrested.

If we burn 1,000 pounds of wheat straw and grain, it will leave 20 pounds of ash; barley, 30 pounds; oats, 40 pounds; rye, 20 pounds, and corn, 15 pounds. This ash represents the proportion of inorganic, or mineral, matter that is contained in the plants mentioned respectively. This proportion must be supplied or the plant cannot thrive, and water in its mechanical and chemical action is the chief factor in providing it. When the rainfall is abundant and seasonal, its meets some, but not all, of these requirements. When it is deficient they must be provided for by irrigation. It may be deserving of remark, in this connection, that the water which descends from the clouds becomes aerated in its passage through the air, and yields needed stores of oxygen and hydrogen, but that is the extent of its contributions. On the other hand, the water that is brought upon the field in ditches, perhaps from great distances, not only supplies the constituents of the atmosphere but also levies tribute upon the soil over which it passes, and pours rich treasure upon the growing crop.

We have mentioned the proportion of inorganic matter that enters into the composition of ordinary cereals. It consists of silica, which is the chemical name for pure flint, quartz, rock crystal, silicious sand and sandstones, aluminia, oxide of iron, oxide of manganese, sulphur, chlorides of potassium, sodium, calcium and magnesium, the carbonates, sulphates and phosphates of soda, lime and magnesia and some other substances. These are ingredients of most soils before their cultivation begins, but in that state water is the agent through which they are fed to the growing plant. It is clear that in their natural state they could not be taken up and distributed through the delicate organs of the stalk and leaves; that can only be effected through the medium of an extremely weak aqueous solution. With every crop taken from a field, there is a reduction of the mineral contents of the soil, until it inevitably occurs that in time they are exhausted, unless they are restored by the application of fertilizers. In regions where farmers depend upon natural rainfall this treatment cannot be deferred after the second year of cropping without a sensible reduction in the yield. Such is not the case with lands that are supplied with moisture by irrigation. They have been known to produce undiminished crops for years without the use of manure or other fertilizers.

This illustrates crudely the advantage of agriculture by means of the artificial appliance of water over that which depends upon the contributions of the clouds, but it does not follow that the former system justifies profligacy to the extent of robbing the soil of what nature has provided for its enrichment. Phosphorus, commonly in the form of phosphate of lime, is an indispensable element of plant growth, and the chief source of supply is the bones of animals. While traveling through the state last fall I saw at numerous points large heaps of the remains of buffaloes piled up by the railway tracks awaiting shipment to the east, and it seemed to me a wretched scheme of money-making. In the course of time the depletion of the phosphates in our soil will be found more difficult to remedy than and other source of impoverishment, and we should preserve such stores as we have with jealous prudence.

We have seen that the carbon which enters so largely into the composition of vegetables is partly absorbed from the air. In most plants, and under ordinary conditions, about an equal portion is extracted from the earth. It is there stored in the form of humus, which consists of decayed vegetable matter. Here there is a very subtle chemistry in operation, in which water is the chief agent. The stubble or straw left upon a field of grain contributes something toward furnishing food for new generations. The carbon in the dead plant in the process of decay must reunite with the oxygen of

the air, to form carbonic acid.   The office of water is here twofold.
The presence of water is an essential condition to the decomposition
of vegetable matter.   When the decay has proceeded so far that
carbonic acid is formed, it is water that conveys it to the thirsting
mouths of the rootlets and so through the various organs of the
growing plant.   Decay is a gradual process, and requires, among
other things, the rays of a summer sun.   So the supply of carbon
that is extracted from the earth is kept up during the season of
growth, but only upon the condition that there shall be a continuous
provision of moisture in the circumjacent earth.   In short, the constituents that enter into the structure of vegetation are or two kinds
—organic and inorganic.   Neither can be provided in a form that
admits of assimilation without the agency of water, and its action
must be timely.   A parched field involves a blighted crop.   It is the
crowning advantage of irrigation that it places it in the power of the
farmer to control his water supply both as to the quantity—for an
excess is harmful—and as to the time.

If we go back to the processes which we have been considering
to the very genesis of the soil, we shall still find water the most efficient factor.   Its action in the disintegration of the rocks is partly
mechanical and partly chemical.   Penetrating the minute pores and
interstices of the granite, the expansion that results from freezing
splits off fragments of greater or less dimensions.   The crumbling
of these pieces is largely the result of chemical agencies.   Water
containing carbonic acid removes the potash from the feldspar and
mica in the form of carbonate of potash, and the same agent separ-
ates the silicate of alumina and the potash.   Thus the rock is resolved into the various mineral substances required for the food of
plants, and water, by its dynamic energy, washes them down from
the mountains into the valleys below.   If upon a thin layer of soil so
formed, seeds of the lower order of plants—lichens, for example—be
deposited, aided by the kindly nurture of the air, they will grow and
fructify.   Their decay will add new elements to the fertility of the
soil and in time fit it to sustain a higher order of plant life.   Later,
animals will be attracted to the spot and by their excrements and
remains contribute still other fertile ingredients until the soil becomes fitted for the highest products.   Such is, briefly and crudely,
the history of the composition of soils.   Their impoverishment commences when they are brought under cultivation, their products removed from the field to serve as food for animals, and they are thus
depleted of their mineral ingredients such as enter into vegetable
structure.

The remark is sometimes heard that agriculture in this section
of the Union can never become the leading industry for the reason
that so much of our area is occupied by mountain ranges.   The answer to this that immediately suggests itself is that it is of little im-
portance if one-half of our territory is unfit for the plough so long as
the other half can produce twice the quantity of crops that are
grown in more level regions.   The difference is due to the fact that
our crops do not depend alone upon the nourishment derived from
the fields that they occupy and the sky above them.   The vast de-
posits of snow in the recesses of the mountains melt beneath the

rays of the summer sun. Their waters trickle in tiny rivulets down the mountain sides, unite in the canyons, and flow in streams through the valleys. Thence they are led by ditches upon new fields of grain, every drop bearing gifts of nutrition. If the late lamented X. Beidler, as he was struggling to build a fire on an intensely cold day, with the only fuel at hand, could say with general optimism, that he "felt sorry for the people in the States, who didn't have any sage brush," surely our farmers can pity their brothers in the east, who carry on their occupation without irrigation ditches. It is by these agencies that we subject to the service of mankind not alone the acres that feel the caresses of the plough, but the adjacent lands, even those that lift their empurpled heights to win and wear throughout the year a diadem of snow.

Upon hearing the above address, it was moved by Nelson of Lewis and Clarke that the thanks of the convention be tendered to Lieut.-Gov. Botkin for his very able address. The vote was carried unanimously.

The president then announced the next order of business to be the discussion of House Bill No. 24. The bill was read by the secretary. It provided for the division of the state into two general departments; the corporate authorities of both departments to be vested in a state water commission; the two members of each department to be appointed by the governor to hold office for two years; each commissioner to receive $4,000 per year salary. Bonds to be voted at an election, to run twenty to fifty years at not to exceed five per cent. interest and not to exceed a half million dollars for the first two years. The commission to have power to condemn canals, flumes, etc., fix the rate of tolls, fix a tax to be collected sufficient with tolls to pay the interest on bonds, and regulate the salaries of employes.

It was moved that Mr. Huffman, author of the bill, open the discussion. The motion prevailed.

Mr. Huffman said:

Mr. President and Gentlemen of the Convention—I am not here as a member of the legislature but as a delegate from Custer county. There are many phases of this bill that I know many of you are better able to discuss than I. There is, however, one purpose respecting the bill at the outset, that I would like to refer to briefly. Now it is well known to all of you who read the papers or talk with your neighbors that for a period of eight years or more no fireside or hotel lobby has been for any considerable length of time free from the sound of this discussion; and about a year ago we thought it was crystallized and that we had agreed; that in most localities in the west private means and private enterprises had about reached the limit of development; that some private enterprises were languishing but that the people in general were more desirous than ever for water; more desirous that our arid lands should have the waters of the state; that we should have more people to patronize our industries. Now I cannot emphasize that latter opinion better than to quote a few lines, which are almost identical with the words delivered by a gentleman who had considerale to say at the late convention: "The first objection to the cession of the arid lands is this, that it is in the interests of monopolists." Now, gentlemen, I am younger than you—the majority of you, but I am not so young as to have been in Montana and witnessed her growth for fourteen years without thinking her mountains are to be developed all alike as soon as possible, and the uses of land and water, to the end that higher inland ditches shall be made possible to the people than we have ever known. Now, if I understand where I am in this case; if I am where I think I am, it is with the people, who want more home-makers, and that they shall be able to enjoy the two elements which have been so ably discussed by our friend, Gov. Botkin.

Mr. Harris said: Mr. Chairman, do I understand by this bill that all the property embraced in the department of irrigation is to be mortgaged or bonded for the purpose of building irrigation canals across the government lands and the lands embraced in this section? As I understood the bill as it was read, I would infer that much. As that bill reads, it subjects all the property of the counties in the department or departments to pay the interest upon the bonds or mortgage which may be issued upon your county, upon your department; and of all the bills that I ever saw or read, that bill is the height of absurdity. The guarantee of the state to the people is its freedom from indebtedness. Of course it is true that before it can become a measure, or can become enacted, it has to be submitted to the vote of the people, but there will be a great many people to vote upon that measure who do not understand it. Every qualified voter can vote upon that act, whether he is a tax-payer or not. Whenever you create a debt in a state you have got to manage in some way to discharge the obligation, and a blanket mortgage is the worst obligation imaginable. I cannot believe a law of that kind will inure to the good of the people.

Mr. Burton—If I understand the meaning of this bill, it is this: The state of Montana is to be divided into two departments, and then those departments shall become the owners of the waters within their boundaries; and those departments proceed as two separate states, as I understand it, which shall have committees to buy all the present water ownership within their respective boundaries and then proceed to build irrigation canals.

I believe I do not mistake the meaning of the bill. Now, gentlemen, irrigation is farming, .pure and simple; irrigation is agriculture and upon the building of irrigation canals in this state a large portion of its future must depend, and the building of irrigation canals is something that every citizen of the state is unquestionably interested in. The statement made that the private enterprises have about reached their height is strange. The private enterprise of this state will be at its height when the millennium comes. Private enterprise is today ready to do the work, ready to do the work of building irrigation canals, wherever they are needed, and wherever anybody can show that they are needed. I am simply giving my view, and if you do not adopt it I am not going to be hurt, and if you do adopt it I am not going to be hurt. But gentlemen, to be serious now, there are two different theories which have been promulgated in this world in reference to government; one of them is old and has been in operation for many centuries, and that is that governments are creatures of the people; there has grown up in the last few years, I may say, this thought, that the people are the creatures of the government. Now, this bill is drawn up upon this new idea. Water is the given heritage of everybody who has to have it. Water is simply a fertilizer and is something that is needed to fertilize the land. We cannot get along without bread in this country, can we? Now, why not include in his bill, to issue bonds and build mills to furnish the people bread, and let the profits of the mill business go into the treasury of the state. Then clothing is another thing that people must have in this country. Then why not sell bonds and go into the wool business and sell the people their clothing. Every argument in behalf of that bill applies in equal force in the flour and sheep business, in favor of this state going into the wool business or the flouring mill business, and as for that matter any other business that the people are engaged in today. It is voluminous; it is something sublime, but the question is, is it practical? I am not a prophet, nor the son of a prophet, but if this bill should become a law there will be no irrigation canals built in this state. Will any man vote a tax upon himself? Will the men all over this state who do not want to see the land taken up vote a tax upon their herds and flocks? It is the worst legislation that I ever saw offered to an intelligent people to adopt. Look at this matter as a business proposition. Is the state of Montana ready to reverse the training and theory that has come down to us, hoary with age? Are they willing to reverse that and to step into building, which will take twenty millions of money? Are they ready to place their names to bonds and mortgages to that amount?

Now, is there any gentleman anywhere that would say that if I or any one were to construct an irrigation canal for a certain amount of water and thus enhance the value of my land, would it be right for the state to take away my property which my money has created? Suppose you don't want to sell your 160 inches of water. They don't want to sell that. Their land is valueless without the water. Now, the state will take away the water from that man, leaving him with his land which is worth perhaps $1.25 or $1.50 per acre.

Mr. Nelson said:

Mr. Chairman- Before I address myself directly to the considering of this bill, I will endeavor to answer some of the statements that have been made by Mr. Harris, and also by Mr. Burton. I think that the statement of Mr. Harris, or rather his objection to this bill, refers especially to that clause which contemplates the taxing of the entire population within a certain district to support the irrigation work to be built in that district. I think that objection answers itself. Certainly that gentleman is aware that there is issued bonds for all sorts of things. The only question is whether it is worth while to issue bonds for the irrigation scheme, or merely vote that the bonds are issued, because we are issuing bonds all the time. The business of this country, as we know, is largely done upon credit all the way through. That certainly is no objection to the bill. I certainly do not think that my friend Mr. Burton, would so presume upon the intelligence of this audience, consisting not only of the irrigation convention, but of a very respectable convention of the house, so far as to stand up here, and having avowed himself an individual of the corporation interested in this very scheme, to then oppose a measure by his language, and by his skilled oratory, which if adopted would enable them to do just what they say they are glad to do.

He was addressing himself to the general provisions of the bill. I do not think he said they would be very glad to sell out. Now, gentlemen, that is pretty thin. Isn't that too thin? I cannot take it in now. A corporation opposing a measure which would enable them to do something which they would be glad to do. We cannot believe that corporations are of that class. He said in the first place that private enterprise in this matter would be at its height when the millenium comes. It will stop pretty short of the millenium. It will stop when the control of the land of the country is with the government. That will be considerably this side of the millennium.

[Reads.] Mr. Powels's theory is that they get the canals too far down the river. Hearn and Carr control 400,000 acres of land. It is not to supply the people with water; it is to get the land. (Mr. Harris states that the state of California has a more humid climate than Montana.)

We must all the time take into consideration all those different things in th.s question. Mr. Burton said another thing. "Will any sane man vote for a tax which doesn't interest him directly?" I think it would be a very short sighted man who would not. I do not know why I should not pay a tax for something by which I am benefitted indirectly. I claim that the irrigation of these lands will in-increase the products of the soil. I have got to eat; I have got to buy those products, and if by increasing the products of the soil I am enabled to buy my provisions cheaper than before; I am benefitted in an indirect way. I find in article 3 section 15 of the statutes of Montana, the organic law of this great commonwealth. [Reads section 15.] The reason why I read this is and the reason why I wish these words to be foundation of what I have already said and what I shall say hereafter, is because of the association in which I find these words. These words I find to be part of what is entitled "A Declaration of Rights," of the people of the State of Montana. Now, gentlemen of the Legislature, it certainly is committed to you to preserve and conserve all the rights of the people of the State of Montana. While there is objections to legislation upon some of these facts, it certainly falls upon you to preserve these rights that are declared to be of public use. Now there are certain ways in which to do it. A settler comes and picks out his place of residence, a place for his home, if he can find such to get out from the storm. A little water is needed by this man for his 40, 80 or 160 acre farm. To supply water to this individual or to those settlers is the duty of the State, and if I am right in law, any special interest, any advantage, I find this declares to be incumbent upon the legislative body of this State, in order to carry out the individual purpose of this constitution. Now, the question is, what does Montana most need today? As in the answer to the old query, "What constitutes a State?" Men, high-minded, noble men. That is what we want in this thing. I say, in regard to this matter, what we need in Montana is an increase in population. We constantly see it in the public press, and the inducements held out by the railroad company induces people to pass through our state every year to the Pacific coast because they cannot find homes here. Forty million acres of arid land. But here is the point gentlemen—those men whom we want here in this State are the farmers who will buy those farms that by these irrigation works have been improved -who will establish their homes here. It was said today that we want more consumers. Those men will inevitably be consumers and they will benefit men like myself as well as themselves. I do want to have more farmers in this State, and I want the lands improved. We want men here who will come out and by their presence and activity increase the industries. Wherever there is gold and silver in the mountains capital is bound to come, but what we want in this State is men, and we cannot have them unless there is some inducements offered.

Now to this bill directly and then I am done. If I am right in my premise, the premise that it is the business of the Legislature, so far as this business is concerned to so legislate, especially if it is their duty, then some such measure should be passed. Mr. Burton said he was not a prophet nor the son of a prophet, but that if this bill passed there would not be any irrigation works made in Montana. I think the gentleman here is making the same mistake. Isn't wholesale cheaper than retail? the small irrigation cost more than large irrigation would?

When a measure of this kind is brought up and people accuse some others of having some sinister motive, mark those people, I am always suspicious of them.

Mr. Harris: I would like to answer Mr Nelson's remarks. He seems to have a great fear. He seems to place Montana in the same climate as the State of California and the south. Today our State is well supplied with cereals. Its supply is nearly equal to its consumption. Just as soon as it becomes profitable for the farmers to raise cereals, then water will be taken from our rivers and the lands reclaimed whenever the enterprise warrants; but as for the State taking hold of this matter in a bill of this kind, it is foolish. Now to show you the weakness of the apprehension of the parties who drew up this bill, I will draw your attention to this part of it. The governor provided that prior to the organizing of a State commission, the governor shall be vested with the corporate organizing as aforesaid, for the purpose of testing the constitutionality of this act. Our State resolving itself into a large corporate body, deems that bill is liable not to be constitutional. For myself I will say that it is not constitutional, that the state has no right to go into a corporation of this kind. As long as we have corporation laws we must expect, as long as they are, we must expect special privileges used by those corporations. Corporations are large bodies without souls. As for this measure, you are creating a corporation out of the whole state.

Mr. Carney said:

Mr. Chairman: About a year ago now, I had the honor of attending a convention of this kind in this city, known as the Irrigation Convention, and as I understood the call of this convention, it was a call upon the farmers of this state to discuss the bill that is now pending before the Legislature, and I believe I have the sentiment of every farmer in this house when I say that I did not come here for the purpose of hearing lawyers discuss it, but they desire to discuss it themselves. I have talked with the gentleman who originated this bill and I believe he is honest and sincere. Whether I believe with him or not, I believe he is honest in his theory, and I would further say that those men who are building canals and tilling the soil are more competent to discuss the methods of building canals and ditches than any lawyer that ever pleaded before a court. My friend, Mr. Nelson, has told you that he wants to get people in here to settle up this country so that he could buy the products of the soil cheaper than he does now. I appeal to you farmers in this country if you can sell your products cheaper than you have in the last several years. You cannot do it and live. Speaking for myself, I have built a canal in company with five others, and we own it and use the water out of it ourselves and we would sooner pay double the expense of keeping up that canal and have the control of the water than be following around a water commissioner that gets a salary of $4,000 a year, and asking him when it would come my turn to get water. While there are some good points in the bill, yet we have got to judge the bill as a whole. We must take the proposition as it presents itself, and I would tonight sit here until tomorrow morning and listen to men who are engaged in tilling the soil, and men who are engaged in building ditches, but I say that I wouldn't spend much time listening to lawyers discuss it, for if I want to go into court I will hire a lawyer.

Mr. Oliver said:

Mr. Chairman: I am nothing but a common farmer, but it is strange to me that a gentleman would get up here and give us a great long talk, yet he deals with no facts whatever. He starts out with the broad assertion that eastern capital would not be brought here to put into irrigation schemes unless they could be assured 15 per cent on their investment. There are lots of ditches built by companies in Colorado, Idaho and in Montana, of which he could see the results of those men who have invested their money in those enterprises, and nothing of that kind is shown. This bill that is under consideration is certainly one that no man who is a farmer that has gone to work and taken the water out and acquired a right to the water of our streams, can ever think of indorsing.

Another speaker said:

I have only a few words to say, and that directly in regard to this bill. Our friend, Mr. Nelson, suggested that we issue school bonds. We do. That is to the benefit of every person who lives in Montana or anywhere else. These bonds are to be given by the State of Montana for the benefit of those who use the ditches and for no other purpose. Now, I have merely a few words to say, a few points in regard to the law in California. The district is composed of people who are benefitted, who receive the benefit of the water, and the bonds are holden upon the lands only, not upon other property. That is not the case with this. All the property in the state of Montana is holden for these bonds. This bill divides the State of Montana into two districts. It taxes the whole State. Then again under this law the taxpayers are at the mercy of the voters. We can get in a lot of laboring men here who want to get us into an immense indebtedness, and we are simply at their mercy. Take a man who has a private ditch, and if I owned a private ditch I would be in favor of the ditch. I think, furthermore, that it is against the constitution of the State. What we need in this State is a law by which we can build and bond ditches.

Mr. Alderson:

The question was raised in regard to taxation. Of course if the bill should pass and the case be submitted to the voters of Montana and the bonds should be voted, provision has to be made for the payment of the bonds, as I understand it, and provision would have to be made for redeeming those bonds on maturity. The proposition is now to taxation of the property of the State. Your law books and merchandise of every description is to be made assessable to pay the interest of those bonds. That is one point. I cannot see where the justice would be of taxing those persons who are already provided with water. I cannot see the benefit of adding an additional amount of tax to those men. It would have a tendency to increase population by offering inducements in some sense to home seekers to reclaim these arid lands, and thus increase the products of the land of Montanan, which might or might not find a market here. Another point I see about this bill, not but that every feature is dangerous. It comes up before the people every two years and is an inducement to the laboring men and the men who want to vote, and they think it is going to open out a great avenue of labor and furnish employment to hundreds of thousands. It will present that inducement for their votes, and especially that portion of the population that controls elections in political matters, and they say, let us go and vote those bonds and after the good times we can go to some other place and let the taxpayers take care of themselves. Gentlemen, I am done for the present.

W. F. Parker:

Mr. Chairman: I felt some little hesitancy about saying anything here this evening, but as this subject has drifted some beyond the discussion of this bill and has involved to some extent the matter of discussion as to whether the State of Montana should attempt to control the water by a general provision of law, I would ike to hear from these farmers upon one subject which has not been spoken of. Mr. Burton, in his water right, takes up all of the water of the Teton. Now, is it the determination of this body and of the State of Montana that there shall never be constructed above Mr. Burton's head-gate a means that shall conserve there the water during the high portion to be conserved there until, say, the months of July and August. Now, suppose the stream of the Teton shall carry 10,000 inches of water, Mr. Burton, in filing his water right, takes nearly all the water of the stream, what right have the men or corporations to go above Mr. Burton's ditches and take the water? Mr. Burton will come in and say that he is entitled to have 20,000 inches of that water, if there is 20,000 inches. If the men shall have no right to the water that flows down there, then you forever prohibit any person from taking it. You give to Mr. Burton a water right that is very valueable. It is this subject of building reservoirs for holding water when it is going to waste until such a time when it shall become necessary in the cultivation of crops. I simply make this as a suggestion, and I would like to hear from the farmers of this district, if Mr. Burton would have more right than he used. If Mr. Burton is entitled to say, 10,000 inches of water, and he has filed a water sight which says he shall have 10,000 inches of water from the stream and somebody goes above him and by means of reservoirs has a water right to his land, can Mr. Burton claim his 10,000 inches of water?

Mr. Harris:

Is that bill up here tonight for passage by this body? I would like to put this motion, that this bill is not taken into the legislative assembly of the State of Montana.

Mr. Myers:

I would suggest that the matter of postponing this bill be deferred until tomorrow morning. I think it is very evident what the sentiment of this body is. I presume that the majority of them are delegates to the irrigation convention, and I think it should not be acted upon tonight. I think that we never will have any use for it and that this convention will be very apt to think that it does not want it, yet I deem that action should not be taken until tomorrow. I move then that the discussion be deferred. The motion prevailed.

The convention adjourned till 10:30 a. m. Friday.

FRIDAY MORNING.

The convention met at 10:30 a. m. A communication from E. G. Brooke was referred to the committee on irrigation law. It was moved and carried that the above committee present a written report.

Reports from the various counties upon the subject of irrigation were then heard. [Reports are printed in the appendix.]

The committee upon irrigation law reported as follows:

Resolved, That this **Convention is opposed** to any legislation at the present time, looking to **the building of** irrigation canals, ditches or reservoirs by **the State from the** revenues of the State arising from taxation. That **we oppose the** issuance of bonds upon the credit of the State **in any form for construction of** irrigation works.

The **majority of your committee recommend that** House bill No. 24 be not **passed.**

> JOHN M. ROBINSON,
> D. M. DURFEE,
> ALFRED MYERS,
> P. CARNEY,
> W. H. SUTHERLIN,
> Z. T. BURTON,
> W. R. GILBERT,
> E. RYAN.

Your committee **is** of the opinion **that there is** further need of legislation **on** irrigation and water **right laws and** ask that they be granted time **in** which **to** draft a bill **covering their** views for discussion by this convention.

> A. H. NELSON, Chairman.

The report **was** discussed by Z. T. Burton of Choteau, W. W. Alderson, B. F. Shuart and others, in favor of the majority report and by A. Nelson in favor of the minority report. The majority report was adopted.

Recess was then taken until noon.

FRIDAY AFTERNOON.

The convention met at 2 p. m.

It was moved that all speeches hereafter made should be limited to five minutes and that no person should speak twice on the same subject save with the consent of the convention.

C. H. Wright, chairman of the committee on constitution and by-laws, reported. The rules were read by sections, amended and adopted by sections, and adopted as a whole.

A resolution was offered by W. M. Oliver, reading as follows:

Resolved, That the legislative assembly of Montana be respectfully requested to enact a law substantially as follows, to-wit:

Sec. 1. That the land commissioner be and is hereby authorized and requested to select and designate, along the streams and ravines of this state, proper sites for reservoirs, and that he shall make report of his selections to the governor of this state with a clear description of the same and that the governor shall make a report of the same to the secretary of the interior of the United States, requesting and recommending that the sites so selected be duly reserved from sale or settlement for the use of the state of Montana.

Sec. 2. That said commissioner is hereby authorized, under the direction of the governor, to employ proper assistants to aid him in making such selections.

Sec. 3. That immediately upon the adoption of this act, it shall be the duty of the governor to send a duly authenticated copy to the secretary of the interior with a request for proper correspondence in regard to this matter and that the said secretary may have a full and respectful understanding of the subject, and asking his co-operation with the state of Montana in this all-important step towards providing for the storage of the waters of the state for the irrigation of our arid lands.

Resolution. were offered by W. W. Alderson, B. F. Shuart and Fred Whiteside, and all were referred to the committee upon irrigation law.

It was moved that the election of officers be the order of business after the report of the committee on legislation at the evening session. The motion prevailed.

A motion to appoint a committee to memorialize congress in the interests of irrigation was lost.

A recess was then taken till 7:30 in the evening.

FRIDAY EVENING.

The convention was called to order at 7:45.

President Rolfe- The first order of business is the report of the committee on legislation.

Mr. Nelson, chairman of the committee—Your committee recommend that the several resolutions referred to it be laid upon the table, with the exception of two of them, which should be adopted as expressing the sentiment of this convention upon the subject appearing in the resolution.

The resolution of W. M. Oliver was then read and placed in the custody of the secretary of the convention.

The committee on credentials said:

Before proceeding further, I desire to have added to the list of delegates from Lewis and Clarke county, the name of Senator W. F. Sanders, who has honored us with his presence here this evening.

By unanimous consent of the convention the name was placed upon the roll of delegates.

The resolution was then taken up. Mr. Nelson having stated in making his report that the first resolution read had received the adoption of all members of the committee and that to the second a minority had dissented, the following remark was called forth:

Mr. President: Before taking up the resolution which the whole committee has not adopted, would it not be better to take up the resolution which the whole committee has adopted?

President—The committee has reported only one resolution.

Senator Sanders—Mr. President: I never heard that resolution before now, but I would like to inquire of the chairman, who is a lawyer and therefore not entitled to say much in this convention. what he thinks of the proposition that the state of Montana owns these waters and is entitled to control them, and that it is not in the situation that it was before we were admitted as a state, when the United States had supreme authority over every stream and could do with it as it chose. Not only have we now become independent of the United States in some things, but with respect to those things that appertain to our sovereignty, supreme over the United States. Of course I understand that the United States has control of all waters that are navigable as waters, and in respect of the land which they own they have a proprietory control of so much of the water as is land; but the state also owns land along those streams, and I think the resolution rather attributes to the United States a little more authority over those streams than it actually has, and until the

United States asserts authority as the owner of land, we have control of it, and I don't know but we have anyway.

Delegate from Silver Bow—From Silver Bow county, I desire to report the names of Lee Mantle, George Irvine and John Caplice, to be enrolled as members of the convention from Silver Bow.

No objection being offered, the gentlemen's names were placed upon the roll.

In response to a call for Sanders, that gentleman said:

I am glad that this subject is open for discussion, because it gives me an opportunity to express my views on the proposition. I will say first, however, that at the former session of this convention my general idea has not been the idea of this convention. My idea and understanding has been that by the enabling act which transferred us from a territorial condition to that of statehood, this state became the owner of the waters—

A delegate—Upon what proposition did it become the owner of them?

Sanders—Upon the general proposition I have just been advancing, that the state is supreme except as to the authority it has surrendered. Continuing what I have to say, without desiring to annoy or harass any gentleman present who does not belong to my profession and therefore must be here in the pursuit of truth, I think that the state is the owner of these waters with the possible modification that the United States owns the land on the banks of these streams, and therefore its proprietory ownership carries with it modified control, which, as it appertains to these lands, might be in case of a non-navigable stream, supreme possession. There is a doctrine of law, of riparian rights; but I understand the United States has abolished or modified riparian rights. This doctrine of appropriation to which the United States itself has conformed, is inconsistent therewith. All I want upon this matter is that you will not act upon the hypothesis that we own nothing. It is a wise judge that amplifies his own jurisdiction and a wise state that takes all it can get hold of. And I believe with reference to these waters that we are entitled to manage them as absolutely as if the United States was no more of an owner than my friend Mr. Holter. In fact, I think he owns about as much land as the United States in this country, and if he doesn't, I know that he is willing to, and that therefore the lands of the United States are subject to our authority somewhat, so far as it has separated its land from its water. I don't recall the exact language of the resolution, but we proceed upon the hypothesis that we are not aliens, and I don't blame anybody on account of it.

Mr. Nelson- If the gentleman will ask for the reading of the resolution, he will find that it pertains solely to the storing of the water, as provided, in certain reservoirs.

Mr. Sanders But why should we run off to the secretary of the interior?

A delegate— The land belongs to him.

Sen. Sanders No; we have a right to control it, and we have a right to occupy it, the United States to the contrary notwithstanding, and it seems to me that it is a pretty good idea to do it—we had rather fight the United States than anyone else anyhow. It don't matter how Jeff Davis came out. I am satisfied that we would come out at the big end of the horn.

The resolution was then re-read and its adoption moved.

Mr. Holter—Before this resolution is acted upon, I would like to inquire of Senator Sanders if there is not a United States law that permits of parties building reservoirs on government land for nothing.

Senator Sanders—I think that is true that parties are author-ized to occupy public lands for that purpose for nothing. That would be included under the ditch right. It doesn't matter how wide the ditch is. A reservoir is a part of the same thing I have no doubt.

Mr. Holter If that be true, what is the use of the resolution? If we have that right already?

Senator Sanders Now, that is a more difficult question.

Mr. Nelson--It is this. The gentleman presenting the resolu-tion desires that this state shall require reservoir sites along the banks of the various streams in the state, so that the state itself may own and control reservoirs for the use and service of the state and lands adjacent thereto, and any individual or individuals within their reach. The law of March, 1891, now gives to individuals or as-sociations of individuals the right to go and take reservoir sites, and upon a plat of it being sent to the secretary of the interior, that land is awarded to such persons. These resolutions look to the acquiring of reservoir sites by the state itself, so that the state may control and own these waters.

The motion carried, and Mr. Oliver's resolution was thereby adopted.

Mr. Nelson—The resolution which was just adopted was report-ed by the unanimous committee. He then read the following reso-lution:

Resolved, That this convention is opposed to any legislation at the present time looking to the building of irrigation canals, ditches and reservoirs by the state, out of the revenues of the state arising from taxation; that we oppose the issuance of bonds upon the credit of the state intended either for the construction of irrigation canals, ditches or reservoirs; and

Resolved, That a copy of these resolutions be sent to the house of representatives and senate of the state.

The adoption of the resolutions was moved and seconded. The ayes and nays were called for. The resolution carried; ayes 25, nays 9.

President—The committee has recommended that the other resolution referred to it shall be laid upon the table.

A delegate—Mr. Chairman, as these resolutions were read before the convention, probably a majority of us are very familiar with them, and if there is no objection, I move that they be laid on the table. Carried.

The chairman of the irrigation law committee reported as follows:

Gentlemen: Your committee on irrigation law beg leave to report that they have considered the list of resolutions and other matters referred to it, and that owing to the short time granted to the committee and the moment of the questions referred to it, your committee has thought it best not to report any law, but recommend that a committee be appointed by this convention whose services shall end with the termination of the present legislative assembly, and that to this committee be referred all bills, resolutions, etc., referred to your committee.

A motion to adopt the recommendation of the committee was amended as follows: That the whole subject be referred to the chairman of this convention, H. P. Rolfe, Hon. W. F. Sanders and Hon. A. M. Holter.

The motion was declared lost and a motion made to appoint a committee to consist of Hon. H. P. Rolfe, Hon. W. F. Sanders, Major Alderson, Mr. H. M. Parchen and Hon. A. M. Holter.

Senator Sanders—I trust my friend will omit my name from the committee and see the propriety of it in a minute.

The name of Mr. Sutherlin was then substituted for that of Senator Sanders; and motion carried.

Burton of Choteau then moved a reconsideration of the vote, which was seconded by Mr. Holter of Lewis and Clarke for the reason that he thought something should be done in the premises and that if left as it now stands it would be dropped.

On motion the motion to reconsider the vote was laid upon the table.

In response to calls, Senator Sanders spoke as follows:

The subject that is before this convention is one of the very largest possible interest. I have never understood that this convention was called or really designed to formulate and specifically define policies with reference to the reclamation of arid lands. The subject is almost as large as maritime or admiralty law—the law which determines the rights of sailors, shippers and vessels upon the sea. We have been giving a great deal of consideration in the congress of the United States to this subject, and a great many gentlemen are very much interested in it. If I were to represent them here and be entirely honest with the gentlemen present, I would say we do not know what to do. We have not been able to arrive at a definite conclusion in this matter. It has been my own fortune to be one of the committee upon the reclamation of arid lands, of which Senator Warren of Wyoming is chairman, and, in absence of knowledge of what ought to be done, what is wisest to be done, and most prudent, we have decided that one thing is pretty safe, and that is, in the first place, to see to what extent we can get the United States to survey the lands and designate the reservoir sites belonging to them. Now, that we will be able to do that, I don't say. I think some portion of it we will be able to do. The United States is engaged in the survey of the public land, and it is also engaged in the designation of reservoir sites, not wholly satisfactory, it is fair to say. A number of gentlemen go and designate reservoir sites as large as a township, where you know, and I know, and the gentlemen sitting in this convention know, there never will be a reservoir and ought not to be. Nevertheless, criticism of these locations and condemnation of them operates to make their action a little more wise. Therefore, we have felt that it was proper that we should continue that examination and location. Of course we have taken the director of the geological survey and shaken him up once in a while, for the reason that we know his action has been unwise. In Montana I have not got the geographical locations in my mind now, but I know if you could see the places designated as reservoir sites, evidently taken in the absence of any close examination in the locality, as for instance, over in Jefferson county there are great areas withdrawn from settlement for reservoirs,—in some a whole township, 36 miles square, designated as reservoir sites. We thought it prudent and justifiable for us to insist that the United States, that owns this large area, might make these appropriations and have these reservoir sites selected, but upon the proposition as to what the people of the state of Montana should do, as to what burdens to take upon the state, or the people of the state, it is a large question. A man might well hesitate about that—first, as to its constitutionality; second, as to its advisability. We all agree that there is no better man on earth than the man who makes two blades of grass grow where but one grew before; and, if we can make a thousand grow where none grew before, that certainly is a benefit which undoubtedly should be consummated. How we shall go about it, what is wisest to be done, is a matter that the most enthusiastic gentleman, the most interested, and the most honest, will confess that he is not entirely competent to determine, but will long hesitate as to the extent that we burden the state of Montana with a public debt, certainly of large dimensions, and forbid immigration. Men will go by Montana if it is largely in debt. They are going by it now, almost uniformly and universally, but if we put a very large and threatening debt on it, they would hardly go through it. The Great Northern and Northern Pacific railroads would fight it as they would pestilence, famine and several other things. [Applause.] There need be no applause about that, because, of course, we all glean from old immigrants in Montana that it is the easiest thing in the world for us to sign our name to a paper and promise that other generations shall pay it, or the incoming migration, but there will not be much migration, for the debt will be large. I know that when a man promises to pay he expects to pay. It is the most convenient thing in the world to sign a note and the most inconvenient to pay it. I appreciate as well as anybody else the proposition that we ought to have these lands rendered fertile, to make garden spots of what is now desert; but I should think that a great commonwealth like this has got to be gradually settled. Everything has got to grow coherently side by side according as it develops, and you cannot go to work and put out a paradise with nobody to occupy it, no angels, male or female, to fly in it. It would be perfectly idle to do so. And while I know of no more beautiful sight than to see the great state of Montana with its wonderful fertility reclaimed by water, even though it is stored, everybody who may come along looking for new lands and new homes will but use it as a stepping stone, if the burden of taxation is likely to be too large. I have sometimes thought that perhaps we should levy a proper tax and reclaim it. That is all right. That is gentlemanly. Take the burden of taxation on ourselves and not palm it off upon our children. The subject is one of great perplexity and magnitude, and if I were to be asked to say what was to be done, I think I would have modestly to say, "I don't know what to do." I came here to find out, but no one has enlightened me, and although we have had several resolutions adopted, I can't say their adoption was wise. I can't say it was foolish. We have for many years endeavored to ascertain to what extent we can enlarge our agricultural area and make it profitable. This only comes down to the ultimate proposition Will it pay? Of course this will pay us if we can get a commission on the bonds, or get into the job; but the big brawny man whose right arm makes Montana beautiful will have it to pay. I am therefore opposed to those who propose to make money off the scheme.

I was much in favor of this convention and the one a year ago, not because I expected you would evolve from them a definite and proper plan that would be wise, because a thing of this vastness can not be settled in a day; it grows up; it is born of thought, not only of wise men, but of all men practical men, and I hope you have not adjourned without getting one step in advance in this matter.

A lawyer is a moral philosopher. If he isn't that, he is a mere chatterer of idle decisions hunting office quite likely. But it is talk upon this matter, I don't mean from lawyers exclusively, or largely, but farmers; but you cannot bar lawyers, merchants or preachers. It is that kind of talk that is going ultimately to evolve out of all this thinking, what is the wisest thing for us to do; and I am afraid you have written a great many resolutions, been up in the Montana club a good deal too much, and sat down here, and haven't talked enough. It is the talk upon this subject of irrigation and what is wisest and best to do, that makes suggestions to you that you are going to take to your homes and talk over with your wives, your neighbors and your children and, when you come here again in six months or a year, that is going to bring out of the whole matter the appropriate thing to do. I can't help you any. I don't know but it is the largest question we have to deal with in the state of Montana. It is precisely as if this convention was coming here now and then to fulfill its mission, adopt rules and regulations, and keep alive the issues and kindle a new interest. That is just what we are to do. In the United States senate and congress we have undertaken so far as we can to turn the matter over to each state for its determination, and let the United States step forward to do what it will. They have had to go moderately at work on it in congress, but the matter has been one of large discussion, and they would like to get rid of it if they could. It is so large that the courts of the United States do not feel adequate to deal with it. One of the ablest and best men in the United States senate said in my hearing, and I believe in response to a speech of my own, that he was in favor of giving the whole thing over to the people of the state and letting them deal with it, and I suppose that is true.

I do not get away from the state of Montana with solicitude for any subject so intense as the solicitude I have about this matter, and I am glad to see that so many men have come from all over the state with the same solicitude; come here with sober minds, not to burden the people of the state, but to take the matter earnestly into consideration and do that which they think to be the wisest and most prudent to the last. This is precisely the condition that devolves upon us, and it is this that alleviates the duty we have to perform in connection with this matter.

A. Nelson spoke of the United States geological survey and reports on canals and irrigation, and referred the delegates to Senator Sanders.

Senator Sanders said only a limited supply of these were given out. He had endeavored to supply the various libraries in the state but could not do much more.

The roll was called preparatory to the election of officers for the ensuing year.

President—The officers of this association consist of a president, two vice presidents and an executive committee consisting of one from each county. The first officer to be chosen is a president.

The names of John A. Robinson of Gallatin and Z. T. Burton of Choteau were then placed in nomination.

Mr. Burton—I feel very grateful for the offering of my name for the honorable position of president of this body, but I was just rising to second the nomination of Mr. Robinson, and I therefore withdraw my name and second the nomination of the gentleman from Gallatin.

Mr. Parchen—I nominate Mr. H. P. Rolfe, the present efficient president of this body.

Mr. Rolfe—I feel very much obliged, but I have had all the honor I desire.

A motion that nominations be closed carried, as did a motion that the secretary be authorized to cast the ballot for John A Robinson for president.

Mr. Robinson was called and responded as follows:

I certainly appreciate the honor which you have bestowed upon me. It was entirely unexpected, and I feel that you have not made a very good choice. Of course, I am not accustomed to making speeches. I never made a speech that amounted to anything in my life; although I have been accused of such things, I plead not guilty. I will certainly do the best I can in promoting the interests of irrigation, and a person **really does not** know what a horse can do until you hitch him up, and certainly when I go home to **the** cares of **my** ranch and the time comes to turn the water on, with a shovel and my sleeves rolled up, I hope **to** be able to promote irrigation.

For first vice president, **Mr.** O'Donnell of Yellowstone **was elected.**

For second vice president, Mr. Wright of Cascade, the secretary casting the vote as before.

Nominations for secretary being in order, Mr. Wade **said:**

Mr. Chairman: The office of secretary, it seems to me, is **the** most important of all, because it is in his hands and in **his power to make this** convention a success. I therefore put in nomination the name of Mr. Robbins, **our present efficient secretary.**

The name of H. M. Parchen was also proposed but withdrawn.

On motion the president **was authorized to cast the vote of the convention for secretary, which he did by casting thirty-six votes for S. B. Robbins.**

Mr. Robbins—I thank you very much for this honor, and I quite agree with **Mr.** Wade **that the secretary will have the** most to do, and I certainly shall do **all** in my power to **promote the** interests of irrigation throughout Montana.

H. M. Parchen was unanimously elected treasurer for the **coming year.**

A delegate—Mr. President: I would like to ask what shall be done in the case of counties not represented; for instance, Fergus county, one of our best agricultural counties, a county where the subject of irrigation requires the most attention, **is not** represented at all.

A voice—Mr. Goodell was in here.

Speaker, continuing—I think there are one or two other counties **that are not represented, and I** merely used that as an example. **What is to** be **done in the** case of new counties created? Members **of the** executive committee, I understand from the rules, are to represent the association in their county and are to rustle around generally, look out for the interests of the society, and particularly to obtain new membership; and it is important that we shall have a representative from every county. We would like some arrangements made providing for representation from each county and also for new counties.

Mr. Nelson—I move that the executive committee that we are to nominate and elect tonight consist of members selected by this convention to secure representatives from the new counties which have been created or will be.

Mr. Oliver suggested that in case of new counties and counties not represented tonight, they could be within the next year entitled to representation by the appointment of citizens of that county who should join the organization.

Mr. Shuart said that he had a little experience in connection with the Wool Growers association of this state. Anyone having work of this kind through the executive committee might correspond with the chairman of the board of commissioners of that county, or with anyone he saw fit, usually some person who first expressed a willingness to become a member of the society; that we take no risk in appointing someone who will accept it.

Mr. Nelson—For instance, say we appoint a man tonight that lives in Choteau county. Being in Choteau county, he will be near Valley county and will know a man in that county to whom he can write, whereas, the secretary would have to write all over the state. The representative of Missoula county will know somebody in Flathead county or the lower county, and so in regard to Teton. If the executive committee will do this, they will save the secretary from writing all over.

By motion duly carried, the president and secretary were authorized to fill all vacancies existing in the executive board after the appointment of members by the convention.

The following members were then chosen: W. M. Oliver, Beaverhead; H. P. Rolfe, Cascade; G. C. Burns, Choteau; A. L. Huffman, Custer; C. K. Hardenbrook, Deer Lodge; Clarence Goodell, Fergus; John A. Keating, Jefferson; W. W. Alderson, Gallatin; Donald Bradford, Lewis and Clarke; W. H. Sutherlin, Meagher; A. G. England, Missoula; Alfred Myers, Park; T. J. Conner, Madison; Z. T. Burton, Teton; Fred Whiteside, Flathead; John Caplice, Silver Bow; Tom O'Hanlon, Valley

Nominations for the engineering committee were then declared in order, and the following were chosen: C. W. Thorpe, Bozeman, Gallatin county; A. J. Crawley, Boulder, Jefferson county; S. B. Robbins, Great Falls, Cascade county; J. M. Paige, Twin Bridges, Madison county; J. W. Wade, Helena, Lewis and Clarke county;

A delegate thought that there had been a motion empowering the president and secretary to receive membership, and was informed that they were authorized by the motion he referred to to fill vacancies in the executive committee.

The following amendment was made to the motion: "And forward the money to the secretary;" which received a second, and carried.

Mr. Wright. of Cascade—I believe the next in order is the selection of a place for holding the next meeting. In behalf of the delegates from Cascade county, in behalf of the board of trade of Great Falls, and in behalf of the citizens of Great Falls, I extend to this convention an invitation to hold its next annual meeting at Great Falls.

The invitation was accepted and the above place designated for the holding of the next annual meeting.

Mr. Wade—I would like to ask for information. If a committee were here to make a certain report and no chairman were named, would the first named be the chairman? Answered affirmatively.

Senator Sanders—Why not make Wade chairman? He is centrally located.

Mr. Wade—I didn't mean that. I simply wanted to know.

President—If there is no objection on the part of the convention Mr. Wade will be appointed chairman of the five engineers.

No objection, and Mr. Wade was declared chairmen.

Moved that a vote of thanks be tendered by this convention to the board of trade and citizens of Helena, and to the several railroads, for favors extended to this convention. Carried.

The president suggested that before adjournment some provision should be made for the publication of the reports and the payment of the bills of the stenographers, of whom, he said, there had been three, during the whole session.

It was moved that the treasurer be required to pay the bills of the stenographers for their reports first, and then if the funds in the treasury were sufficient, to have printed 500 copies of the proceedings, that a copy thereof be furnished to each member of the convention, and that the rest be judiciously distributed throughout the state. Carried.

It was suggested that someone should arrange the reports and get them in proper shape for publication. The president said there were yet some reports to be received; that that from Park county was the only one in shape to go into the pamphlet; that it would be necessary for someone to arrange the pamphlet before publication.

The following motion then carried:

I move that the secretary compile the pamphlet, and if there is sufficient money in the treasury, to have it published, and that he also be instructed to purchase for his use suitable stationery.

The question of the cost of publication was taken up and the matter of the same expense last year discussed.

The secretary was instructed to correspond with Mr. Brown, the chairman of the printing committee, on the subject.

Mr. Nelson—I move that the person who was treasurer of the last convention be requested by the secretary upon the action of this convention to report in full how much money was received and how much expended, and let it be embodied in the proceedings of this convention; and that he turn the balance, if any, over to the new treasurer of this organization. The motion prevailed.

A motion was introduced that the secretary of the committee on publication be required to give an account of the money and state how many pamphlets were distributed and turn over the balance of the money, if any, after having made his accou ting, which of course was to be accompanied by the printer's bill. Carried.

Mr. Nelson said he understood that the constitution made no provision for a report by the treasurer so far as this convention is concerned, and thought provision should be made for a report at the next annual meeting by the treasurer of all money received and expended —make a full statement of the accounts of the convention.

A motion to the effect that the minutes of this meeting be published; that 500 copies be put in the hands of the executive committee for distribution according to some equitable means, was introduced.

President—I want to say that in the manner in which these papers are today, the secretary will have to employ a typewriter in order to get them into shape, and he ought to be compensated for the expense.

Mr. Burton of Choteau moved that the motion just introduced be amended to the effect that the secretary see that the publication of these proceedings did not cost more than the amount of money in the treasury. Amendment concurred in and motion carried.

Senator Sanders—I move that the thanks of this association be tendered to the officers of this convention. Carried.

Mr. Whiteside—I listened with a great deal of interest to the remarks made tonight by our senator, and while I do not feel able to follow him, I wish to express one or two thoughts that occurred to me as he was talking. He said he hoped this convention would not adjourn without taking one step forward in the solution of this problem of irrigation, and I do not see that we have. While I agree with him in everything that he said, most particularly in the statement that this subject is a vast one, and while it is vast and the responsibilities are great, it is certainly not a new one. It is the same condition that confronted the people of Colorado, California and other states, and while they have not solved the problem entirely, they have certainly gone forward on the line; and I move you that the officers of this convention be a committee, together with the president and secretary, the two vice presidents and three of the executive committee whom they shall appoint, shall be a committee to frame or suggest to the legislative assembly of the state of Montana suitable legislation.

Mr. Murray of Gallatin—I have been working with the Farmers alliance of Gallatin county, but on a different proposition than this. I have learned from Senator Sanders that he was not able to solve or tell the people what was the best way to pursue to alleviate the ranchmen and farmers of the great state of Montana from the dilemma which legislation or rather, lack of legislation, has placed the honest yeoman of Montana. You contravene the interest of the farmer of today when you license corporations to take water from the rivers of Montana; and when you take away from the honest yeoman and the people and place the water in the hands of a corporation, you rob them; you rob the beef raiser; you rob the sheepman; you rob the horseman; you rob the miner who takes gold and silver out of the bowels of the earth, because you emburden upon him a higher price for everything he uses. I have a bill here of the prices of the farmer's products of Gallatin valley and the state at large, that I dare any man to contradict as far as its veracity is concerned, and you can go home and figure for yourselves and see what the farmers of the state are getting for what they produce. Now, we get 50 cents a bushel for wheat (flour is worth $2.20 now), oats are worth 80 cents and potatoes 60 cents a hundred. Now I ask this convention that they frame a law and that they frame that law to stop corporations from taking the water from the honest yeoman.

Senator Sanders concurred in the propositions advanced by Mr. Murray. He said the gentleman was right. It would be a good deal wiser to say we won't have any corporations in the state or any other thing that is an outrage and no more upon everybody. If a man wants to go into business, let him take his money and go into it; let him take his credit and go into it; let him take his individual liability and go into it. That is all right; he then becomes the indorser of his enterprise; he is responsible for his success or failure; his estate is security that he won't run around and undertake swindling anybody; but we have enlarged this matter of incorporating any enterprise until we have encouraged this gambling into every line of business, and with $500 or $1,000 a man can set up any kind of game he chooses under the guise of a corporation and cheat anybody and leave him a creditor of his concern. If he has made out of that corporation five hundred or more dollars, he can laugh at owing any widow or orphan in the state and every farmer, and can walk off with the money, and they have no redress. So that, if the people of Montana apprehend the philosophy of government as philosophers, we can incorporate railroad companies because that we all feel is a public convenience, but when it comes down to extending the laws of corporation to business affairs, if permitted at all, he thought ample security should be given that the business be conducted honorably; that business corporations would exist and the farmers and the people of Montana continue to be swindled by the shrewd, deceiving and dishonest incorporators until their eyes were opened and proper legislation secured on the corporation laws of the state.

He referred to the common law on the subject of corporations, saying that it extended the privilege of incorporating only to those concerns which were of public convenience, as railroad and gas companies. To that he was favorable. But while he thought that the privilege of incorporating was properly given them, street railroads, water, gas and electric light companies, he said, should be under the control of the state and the people of the state; that if a man wanted to enter into any business, let him take his money and invest it on his own liability; if he succeeds, he is justly entitled to his profits; but if he fails, make him give up his estate and every part thereof until every man, woman and child who are creditors of his are paid. Corporations had fed on the people for the last twenty-five or fifty years and made the Goulds, the Vanderbilts, the Astors and the Westinghouses.

In conclusion he said that though the appointment of a committee, as suggested by Messrs. Whiteside and Murray, was all right, he did not know what kind of a law they would frame; that it should be one declaring the water of the state the property of the state and the people of the state and the land along the banks a part and parcel of the sovereignty of the state of Montana. He referred incidentally to Mr. Parchen whom he said was a member of the gas company. He was in favor of paying him for his plant and letting it be the property of the people of the state—the property of the public.

The following resolution was introduced:

That the executive committee, together with the president and secretary, be instructed to draw up resoluitons on this question, to be presented at the next session of the body at Great Falls.

To which the following amendment was made:

That the secretary be instructed to send to every member of this society a copy of the proposed bill or proposed resolution, at least thirty days before the convening of the next convention.

The amendment was accepted and the motion carried.

Mr. Murray suggested that the president and secretary and executive committee, forming the committee just chosen, should have Senator Sanders' aid in drawing up the resolutions.

President Rolfe—You have elected a president, and I think it is but fitting that he take the chair before we adjourn; and I appoint Messrs. Wade and O'Donnell to conduct Mr. Robinson to the chair.

A motion was introduced to the effect that the president, two vice presidents and secretary be a committee to arrange a program, employ speakers, etc., one month before our next annual meeting for the purpose of reading before the convention at that time.

The motion carried.

It was suggested to the president that he might possibly not have looked over the rules as yet, and that there were to be representatives, one from each county, appointed to prepare papers and reports to present to the convention at its next meeting and that they be men who are superintending ditches, practical men, and not those entirely ignorant on the subject.

On motion of H. P. Rolfe the convention adjourned sine die.

REPORTS ON THE STATE OF IRRIGATION IN SEVERAL COUNTIES.

CASCADE COUNTY.

In Cascade county the record for irrigation is as follows:

Sun River, in operation, 12 miles, approximate cost, $24,000; Crown Butte, 26 miles, $76,000; Wilson & Thomson, 24 miles, $70,000; Chestnut Valley, 12 miles, $24,000; Missouri Rapids, 5 miles, $15,000; Willow Creek, 7 miles, $7,000; Muddy, 10 miles, $10,000. Total, 96 miles, $226,000.

Under construction—Benton lake, 20 miles; Priest's rapids, 24 miles; Muddy reservoir, 217 acres area, average depth 25 feet, to cover about 4,000 acres in connection with the Muddy ditch, to cost, approximately, $10,000.

Small ditches, owned with the land and built at a comparatively limited cost, as follows, from one to three miles long: Belt creek, Willow creek, Otter creek, Sand Coulee creek, Deep creek, Wegner creek.

One great drawback upon irrigation today is the system of taxation. Example: A ditch 10 miles long, costing $10,000, to irrigate 2,000 acres, assessed $6,666; 2,000 acres of land assessed $30,000; 2,000 acres adjoining land assessed $30,000, making total assessment $66,600, less adjoining land assessed at $3 per acre, $12,000, leaving assessment on the ditch, which cost $10,000, at $54,600, and this two years before a drop of water had been put through the ditch.

Taken as an example of whether irrigation pays or not, the strip

of the Sun river valley from Great Falls to the town of Sun River
shows without any assistance from other sources. From the mouth
of the river to where the Muddy empties in the valley is given up to
prairie dogs and nothing is raised. This stretch is about fifteen
miles long. When one goes up the hill at Sun River Leavings, what
a sight meets his eyes, and how entirely different from the one just
left behind ! Ahead, the valley is green with great fields of timothy
up to one's waist, fields of wheat thrashing forty and often more
bushels per acre, oat fields where the farmer gets his eighty bushels
per acre and more, avenues of trees along the roads and up to the
houses, the farms fenced, well-built houses and good barns, sometimes of stone, and every evidence of prosperity, and the whole of
this caused by a little stream of water running a distance of twelve
or thirteen miles in a ditch about ten or twelve feet wide, and applied
to the farms along its course. One of the most noticeable places is
that of Mr. Robert S. Ford, the president of the Great Falls National
bank, and he was laughed at when he started in to reclaim this un-
promising piece of land, all covered with sage brush twenty years
ago when he took it up, and now one of the prettiest places in the
state and a profitable one too.

Cascade county has the water and the land, more water than
almost any other portion of the arid region, and land second to none,
and what is needed is capital to go ahead and wise energetic men at
the head of the enterprises to build the canals and colonize the lands
under them.

The greatest drawback to the proper development of the arid
region is the building of small ditches along the bottom lands, using
up the water and wasting it so that there never can be water enough
to put into a high-line canal without endless lawsuits, and probably
not then. But if the high-line canal (and there is almost always one)
were built first all these small ditches would be unnecessary; their
owners could get water from the big ditch just as well, without the
loss of available water from seepage and evaporation caused by all
the small ditches. The bench lands are almost invariably the best
adapted for agriculture and these could be developed by a high-line
canal where they never could be reached by the small ones. Right
here in Cascade county and the adjoining portions of Teton, Lewis
and Clarke and Choteau, that are in the same drainage basin, lie
about 1,000,000 acres of unexcelled agricultural land that could be
watered by the building of two systems of irrigation canals. The
two systems would cost very large sums of money, but they would be
cheaper than the average of the United States by many dollars when

the cost per acre irrigated was considered. But they would support a population of half a million people, directly and indirectly. They would be paying propositions to the promoters, the investors, the farmers, and to the whole state of Montana.

"Irrigation has been waiting to receive the same enthusiastic consideration that the men of the west have lavished upon mines, town lots and railroads. If Colorado, Montana and Utah will put their brains and energies into the subject now they will go to the front with a bound."

GALLATIN COUNTY

Gallatin county was one of the earliest settled counties in the state and the farmers started in in early days to construct ditches and there are now some sixty-four or more ditches, some very expensive, almost all of them completed. Irrigation can show in Gallatin county the best practical results of any county in the state, if not in the entire arid regions. Such in fact was the expression of Senator Stoddard when, as a member of the congressional commission, he visited Montana three years ago.

Most of the canals and ditches have been constructed by private enterprise, paid for by local capital, and principally by the farmers. I think it is safe to say that they have expended since the settlement of the county $500,000 in canals and irrigating ditches, four-fifths of which have been constructed by the farmers themselves. There are two ditches which are under the control, practically, of outside capitalists, but one of which has been constructed by outside capital. In fact, they cannot be said to be controlled by outside capital, as the parties who have contributed most extensively are the farmers in Gallatin valley.

The Manhattan Malting company has the most expensive ditch in the county if not in the state. The main ditch is twenty-four miles in length and they propose to add three miles, making twenty-seven miles in all, which will cost $100,000.

The Gallatin canal was started by the farmers themselves, but they felt as though they were unable to complete it so they appealed to outside capitalists, who induced the farmers to take stock in the enterprise and they managed the business. The farmers took almost stock enough to build the ditch and the matter is now in the courts. It seems that the incorporators and officers of the ditch company voted to themselves a large amount of stock with no consideration while the stock that was issued to the farmers had to be paid for, in actual work on the ditch. I see that the courts have recently set aside the action of the incorporators and officers of the company, so far as they have appropriated large blocks of stock to themselves and to which they were not entitled, so that, practically, the canal, which is eighteen or twenty miles in length, and cost $75,000, was built by the farmers of the Gallatin valley and it will eventually fall into their hands.

The ditches there are easily constructed and the valley is beautifully watered, as every one knows. It is comparatively easy to divert the water of the streams on to the land to be irrigated. It is merely a matter of sticking in a plow and plowing a few furrows which are cleaned by the use of some crude instrument to throw out the dirt, but whatever sort of a ditch it is they all cost money. With the ditches we now have, perhaps one-half of the tillable land is under ditch, or can be irrigated.

There is another ditch there called the Excelsior. It was built in six or eight months and I do not know what the cost was. It is proposed to increase the length of this ditch the coming season. We have had more or less litigation at first to quiet the rights of the claimants to water and to determine the amount of water each of the parties is entitled to. This has amounted to a considerable amount of money in the aggregate, but it has been distributed amongst so many that it has scarcely been felt.

At present we are in splendid shape in regard to the condition of our irrigating ditches and canals. We are producing a large amount of grain in the Gallatin valley and in the foothills next to the mountains and on the mountain slopes thousands upon thousands of bushels of winter wheat have been raised without resorting to irrigation. This land will remain as fertile and sustain large crops, as it has been demonstrated that our mountain streams furnish, very largely, the necessary ingredients to sustain and restore the soil and supply that which was taken away by the crops. The soil varies in depth from six to eight feet. Our irrigation system has demonstrated that where the ground has been properly cultivated and irrigated for one or two years it needs a less amount of water afterwards than it did at first. I have noticed very frequently that after a severe dry spell irrigation causes a heavy rainfall. There may be something in the statement that the evaporation of the water causes condensation. There does not seem to be so much trouble about water as in former years. Our farmers do not resort to irrigation so often in the season to produce their crops. It is seldom that they have to irrigate more than once or twice, unless it is where the soils are somewhat shallow with boulders and gravel near the surface. There is a great diversity of soil in the Gallatin valley. A portion of this has been taken up by the Manhattan Malting company. It is sandy and loose and requires more water than moist soil. It has been demonstrated that it produces excellent barley. They will raise 30,000 bushels and will add very largely to the productive industries of Gallatin county. They are becoming quite an important factor in our prosperity.

JEFFERSON COUNTY.

Jefferson county is situated about the center of the state. It has quite an amount of agricultural land and is watered largely by the Missouri river on the southeast, and the Big and Little Boulder rivers, White-tail Deer creek, Cataract creek, Muskrat creek, Basin creek, Red Rock creek, Elkhorn creek, Beaver creek, Big and Little Pipestone creeks, Fish creek, Crow creek and Prickly Pear creek.

Along all these streams is a large area of agricultural land, only partially covered by water. There are about two hundred and twenty-five miles of what is known as irrigating ditches taken from the above named streams, carrying all the way from twenty to five hundred inches of water each, and irrigating about thirty-four thousand acres of land during the wet season, but during the dry season about one-third of the above number would be useless.

There is, with the exception of extreme dry weather, a sufficient supply of water to fill all the ditches. But by the construction of small dams on the above creeks, there could be water enough saved to cover four times that amount of land.

Speaking of dams and reservoir sites, would say that nature has placed good sites on all these streams, not requiring dams of over fifteen to three hundred feet in length. These would furnish water enough to cover all the agricultural land along these creeks.

Very respectfully,   E. RYAN.

PARK COUNTY.

Park county has an estimated acreage of 130,000 acres of agricultural lands, something over 40,000 acres of which are under irrigation. Her source of water supply is the Yellowstone river and its various tributaries, the largest and principal ones of which are Shields river, Big Timber creek, Sweet Grass creek, the Boulder and the Clark's fork, the latter bringing in the waters of Red Lodge and Rocky fork **creeks.**

Our county was first occupied exclusively by stock growers, and used as one vast range. The stockmen paid no attention to the raising of any crops other than hay, and depended on the Gallatin valley for their grain and vegetables. The building of the Northern **Pacific** railroad and the consequent building up of towns along this line created a demand for farm products that induced men to test the capacities of the soil, and the raising of grain and vegetables of all kinds was found so profitable that all the land that can be watered cheaply on the upper Yellowstone and Shields river is at present under cultivation, and Park county's stock-growing interests are now second to her agricultural. Gradually the ranch hunter has pushed up the smaller streams locating the valley and bottom lands, till the latter ones have been forced to the bench lands, which are now, well up to the foot of the mountains, under the influence of water, and there we find today our most valuable farms and by far the greatest yields. To the present time the most of our farming has been done on the valleys and small streams where the settler could build his ditch quickly and at small expense. The waters of these streams being almost all appropriated and the demand for farm products far in excess of the supply, some of our more enterprising citizens have been induced to construct expensive ditches from the Yellowstone river to irrigate the valleys and bench lands adjacent thereto, which could not be reached by the water from the smaller streams. The year 1892 has witnessed the construction of a ditch fifteen miles in length, carrying 6,000 inches of water, to irrigate the valley in the upper Yellowstone; two ditches between Livingston and Mission creek bringing some 6,000 acres of land under the wholesome influence of irrigation, thus converting table land almost worthless into valuable farms. Another ditch some ten miles in length is carrying 10,000 inches of water from Big Timber creek into the fertile and productive valley of Otter creek. These three large ditches are all that Park county can boast of today.

The valley of the Boulder has most all been taken up and placed under irrigation by small ditches, but the bench lands on both sides of the river have not yet felt the influence of irrigation, and only await the construction of canals too expensive for the individual farmer to build to bring under cultivation farms more extensive than are now under cultivation, in the bottoms and valleys.

A visit to the upper Sweet Grass valley reveals the most prosperous of all Park county farms. These lands are watered by small mountain streams from which ditches have been constructed at little expense, but here again are the bench lands lying idle for lack of capital to construct irrigating canals.

The southeastern portion of Park county has only recently been brought to the attention of agriculturists by the opening of the Rocky fork coal mines, and the construction of the Rocky fork railroad. Here we find the Red Lodge and Willow creek valleys, that are second in fertility to no portion of the United States. These valleys comprise 50,000 acres of land that must for the most part be irrigated from the waters of the Rocky fork creek, but canals for this purpose can not be built at a cost within the means of the settlers and ranchers. For this purpose capital will have to be called upon, or state aid obtained to help build the necessary canals and ditches. That portion that can be watered by the smaller streams is now taken up and being cultivated, but hundreds of valuable locations are awaiting the building of canals only, when they will support large and prosperous communities.

Park county successfully grows all kinds of small fruits and apples of the hardier varieties; oats from forty to eighty bushels per acre; wheat of a good quality twenty-five to fifty bushels to the acre; barley not excelled anywhere; potatoes and all other root crops in such enormous yields that we hardly dare give the actual figures, as strangers to our soil could not believe them true. It is only with the aid of irrigation that any of our land is productive, and if some equitable system can be devised whereby the state can render us any assistance it will certainly add millions to the wealth of the state of Montana. We need not fear overproduction so long as the state imports from older states millions of dollars' worth of farm products annually. A market can be found for all we can raise at home.

T. P. McDonald.

MEAGHER COUNTY.

Mr. Sutherlin stated that the report from Meagher county would be similar to the report presented last year, except that we have made considerable progress with our irrigation in Meagher county. The proposed ditch or canal spoken of in that report has been put into operation, that is, a company has been organized and nearly all of the stock has been sold. The company has spent about three months in constructing a canal four or five miles in length. Its machine for ditching is one of the most improved (I have forgotten the name of it) and it does the work admirably. It is proposed with this canal to cover the portion of Meagher county that remains uncultivated. I believe the canal will be a great thing for the Missouri valley. It will be the making of Broadwater county—make it one of the best agricultural districts in the state. The entire bench lands along the valley are good and will produce great crops. This has been proven by tests already made. I look to see great results from that canal.

In the Musselshell there have been several canals taken out within the last year or two. These have taken about all the water of the river. The longest of these canals is about seven miles long and carries about 800 inches of water. The other is probably four miles and carries the same amount of water.

TETON COUNTY.

One of the oldest canals is the Eldorado, which covers an area of about 15,000 acres of land, obtained by several parties upon speculation, which is non-productive at present. This canal carries about 150 cubic feet per second. The largest canal in this county is the Eureka, about forty-two miles in length, including main and main laterals, carrying about 250 cubic feet per second, covering an area of about 30,000 acres, of which about 12,000 acres have been filed on. Both of the above canals receive their water from the Teton river.

There are several small canals tapping the various streams in the entire county, making a total length of over 200 miles. Within this county there are at least 100,000 acres of land under these canals the greater portion of which would be purely grazing lands were it not for artificial watering. At present the so-called natural hay lands are almost a failure and every stockman we meet says we will have to make canals on our lands to insure us plenty of hay to winter our stock.

It is universally acknowledged that irrigation is the only means by which the demands can be supplied. On our desert lands with canals eighty bushels of oats per acre have been raised. Wheat and barley are looking well and promise an excellent yield at this date. Bluejoint hay has proven quite a success on the Basin and Eureka ranches. All herbs and   etables grow in abundance in this entire county.

Some companies claim that irrigation will not pay in northern Montana, but a close investigation and observation have revealed the fact that their claim is based upon experience with canals poorly constructed, on uneven grades, which wash in some places and fill up in others, so that the repairing costs more than the actual irrigation of grain and grass; also the manager sends men out that never saw a ditch before and does not instruct them by going personally on the ground, and the next time the water is turned on he has another new man and sends him out in the same manner as before. These men let the water run too long in one place, then the land gets too dry and crusts, and the result is a poor yield of grain or half of a crop of hay. Irrigation has to be conducted on scientific and business-like principles.

What would be the result if a merchant, a bank or a manufacturing establishment changed employes every week or month? It would not pay; they would close up. As it has been in the past, the markets have been distant from most of the fine agricultural lands, but today railroads bring them within easy reach of all valleys, which should insure economic farmers a fairly good profit on grain. Irrigation will make these bench lands graze at least ten head of stock to where they will now graze one without water.

Another detriment to the cause is that many engineers have induced capitalists to invest money upon certain statements which could not be verified and they put in large sums of money, but their plant finally cost three or four times the original estimate. Water is often carried past choice lands a long distance to other lands and seepage is so great that but a small portion of the water gets to the land. The final true conclusion is a non-paying investment. I honestly and sincerely submit my opinions based upon actual experience for the consideration of those interested in irrigation.

Very truly,   M. F. ALLEN.

YELLOWSTONE COUNTY.

There is practically an unlimited supply of water for irrigation in that portion of the Yellowstone valley tributary to Billings. In Yellowstone county there are exclusive of the recently acquired strip of the Crow reservation 1,500,000 acres of irrigable land, of which 500,000 are now under ditch. All of the larger ditches are taken out of the Yellowstone river. The largest is that owned by the Minnesota and Montana Land and Improvement company, which is forty miles long. It is controlled by the heirs of Frederick Billings and Freeman Clark. It is a high line ditch and there are 60,000 acres of first-class land under it, one-half of which is under cultivation, but principally in hay. Other ditches are the Canyon creek, twenty-eight miles long, in the center of the valley, owned by a syndicate of farmers; Italian ditch, fifteen miles long; Mill ditch, company, fifteen miles long; Clark's Fork Ditch company, ten miles; Yellowstone Ditch company, fifteen miles; Stillwater ditch, twelve or fifteen miles; the McAdow ditch, six miles, and a large number of smaller ones, the latter covering about 30,000 acres of land. All these ditches, save that of the Minnesota and Montana company, are owned by farmers' syndicates, each share of stock entitling a farmer to an inch of water. The river has a fall in the vicinity of Billings of ten to fifteen feet to the mile, while the fall in the ditches is about three feet to the mile. The advantage the Yellowstone valley farmer has over the eastern agriculturist lies in the fact that he never has to fertilize his land. The river carries in its current fertilizing material; the ditches, having less flow than the river, catch the fertilizer and carry it on the land. It takes three years to get a first-class crop, and at the end of ten years' constant use the soil is more fertile than at the end of three. The most productive ranches in the valley are those that have been cropped the most often, and not a dollar has been spent in fertilizing.

A few illustrations will show how profitable farming is in the Yellowstone country, and how successfully mixed farming can be carried on. The first man to experiment with the raising of alfalfa in Yellowstone county was B. F. Shuart. In 1883 he took up 640 acres of land near Billings under the desert land act, and with no previous experience in farming and a capital of less than $500 he began. He devoted his attention wholly to crop raising until 1887, when he bought a band of sheep and began feeding them alfalfa. In May, 1892, he sold ranch, buildings and stock for $40,000. The foundation of his success was his ability to raise alfalfa and feed it to his sheep. In 1881 the farmers within twenty-five miles of Billings had a surplus of 3,000 tons of hay. This they sold at $15 a ton, bringing the farmers in that small radius $45,000 cash. It cost them $3 in the stack and $3 to bale and deliver at the railroad, leaving a net profit of $9 a ton. The next year the market for hay was a poor one; instead of shipping they bought small bands of sheep, fed them the surplus, and by utilizing the hay in this way they made the surplus hay worth to them $22 a ton in mutton and wool. In the last five years the value of irrigated land has risen from $5 to $30 an acre in the county. The largest farm in the county is that operated by Bailey & O'Donnell, containing 5,000 acres. It is mixed farming on a big scale, for in addition to large crops of grain, hay and vegetables, they run 7,000 or 8,000 head of sheep, and are extensive cattle and horse growers. Mr. O'Donnell is a practical farmer, and is the superintendent of the Minnesota and Montana Land and Improvement company. He is thoroughly conversant with everything in connection with irrigation, having made a study of the systems in Utah and Colorado. He is among the successful Yellowstone farmers.

Statistics carefully kept for the last three years show that with ordinary care and industry every cultivated quarter section of land in the valley will yield a net annual profit of $1,000. This is on the basis of what has been raised, and not what might be produced in addition. The dairy interest as well as poultry raising is almost entirely neglected, notwithstanding the fact that thousands of dollars are sent out of Montana into Nebraska, Iowa, Kansas and Utah each year for butter, eggs and chickens. Hog raising could also be successfully carried on by the Yellowstone farmer. They do splendidly on alfalfa, the climate is all right for them, and a profitable market is always assured.

Some time ago the Crow Indians ceded to the government 2,000,000 acres of their reservation, and this is now open to settlement. It is on the north side of the river from Billings and contains some of the best land in the state. Five hundred thousand acres can be irrigated. Already numerous filings have been made upon it, but there are homes there for hundreds of families. These 500,000 acres are well watered by small, swift streams that have their source in the mountains. There is a running stream on every mile or two of the land, so that it will be necessary to build only short and comparatively inexpensive ditches to utilize it. The streams on the Crow reserve, like the Yellowstone, are highest in July and August, just when they are most needed, because they are fed by the melting snow high up in the mountains. In addition to the land acquired from the Crows, and the unoccupied land in the Yellowstone valley, there are 1,000,000 acres of good agricultural land in what is known as Lake basin. This basin is thirty miles north and south by 100 east and west. It is a natural depression, surrounded by hills. There is a large shallow lake in the vicinity which offers an excellent opportunity to irrigate a large portion of this basin. Lines run by representatives of the United States geological survey showed that a high line ditch, 125 miles long, could be built, which would cover a great portion of it, and that the cost of the canal would not exceed $10 an acre. One-half of the land the ditch would cover is owned by the Northern Pacific railroad and could be purchased for $2.50 to $3 an acre; the rest could be taken up under the desert land act, 320 acres by each settler. A company building such a ditch and buying the railroad land could sell sufficient of it to settlers at $10 an acre to pay for the construction of the canal and still have the water for sale. As irrigated land is worth $20 to $30 an acre within three years after the water is put on it, it will be seen that there is a chance for profit in the enterprise both for the company and the settler. A small area could be covered at a cost of $250,000.

BEAVERHEAD COUNTY.

Beaverhead county is geographically located in the southwestern portion of the state and well up on the slope of the Rocky Mountain range. It is a mountainous district with an area of about 4,500 square miles. Of this area about 800,000 acres is surveyed land and may be classified as follows: 200,000 acres farming land; 300,000 acres hay and grazing land; and the balance "upper bench" land, suited only for sheep grazing. Over 180,000 acres have been reclaimed under the different land laws and final proof made thereon, as shown by the records of the Helena and Missoula land offices; and the great bulk of this land is now kept in a state of reclamation and productiveness by the process of irrigation. However, to attempt to give the mileage of the private ditches and their laterals covering a vast quantity of land, in a report of this kind, would be exceedingly difficult, and our readers must draw on their imaginations for conclusions. The county is traversed by the following streams, which furnish the water for irrigation in the valleys in which they are located, to-wit: The Beaverhead, Blacktail, Rattlesnake, Grasshopper, Horse Prairie creek, Medicine Lodge creek, Trail Creek, Sage creek, Big and Little Sheep creeks, Painter creek, Birch creek, Willow creek, Rock creek and Big Hole river. Of all these streams the Beaverhead is the most important, as the valley of that stream is the principal agricultural valley in the county. There are now about 20,000 miner's inches of water claimed in this stream and being used for irrigating purposes in the Beaverhead valley, 7,500 inches of which is claimed by the Canyon Ditch Co., Union Ditch Co. and Beaverhead Canal Co. in about equal proportions, and the balance by private individuals. The valleys of these streams are for the most part at too great an altitude to be used for agricultural purposes, having an average altitude of about 5,000 feet.

During the average water season there is a supply in the Beaverhead more than sufficient to fill all ditches already constructed, but during dry seasons such as 1889 and 1890 there was not enough to supply present demands, and many claimants suffered on account of shortage; and what is true of Beaverhead in this respect is also true of every other stream in the county except the Big Hole river. In fact the waters of all other streams in the county except the latter are fully appropriated, and the contests over water in our courts in later years fully prove this.

The state (through our land commissioner) has selected —————— acres of "table lands" in Beaverhead valley, on the bench west of the Beaverhead river, and it is apparent to everyone acquainted with the condition of irrigation in the county that before these lands can be made available something like the storage process must be resorted to. During the high water seasons the amount of water that flows past us on its way to the ocean might and should be utilized by being turned into reservoirs for the purpose of supplying future demands.

I am of the opinion that every acre of arid land in this county can be reclaimed by constructing dams at the outlets of the lakes on our streams. During the dry seasons of 1889 and 1890 I was short of my usual supply from Rock creek. During the winter of 1890-91 I constructed a dam twelve feet high at the first lake to retain the waste water, thus giving me a body of water one-half mile wide and more than a mile in length. Should this not prove sufficient I can build dams at the outlets of other lakes higher up the stream. Where there are no lakes it is not difficult to find flat or marshy places where a dam can be constructed at a nominal expense with timber, rock, gravel, etc. This work can be done during the winter months.

JOE A. BROWN.

BARNARD BROWN'S REPORT.

HELENA, Mont., Feb. 22, 1893.

Messrs. H. P. ROLFE, President and S. B. ROBBINS, Secretary,
    Great Falls, Montana:

Gentlemen: Agreeable to your communication of the 20th inst.,
I submit statement of the receipts and disbursements of the Printing
committee of the Irrigation convention as follows:

RECEIVED.

From Deer Lodge, Dawson, Lewis and Clarke, Custer,
    Gallatin, Silver Bow (per W. A. Clark), Missoula,
    Meagher, Fergus, Park, Madison, Cascade, Jefferson
    and Choteau counties—14 counties—$100 each $1,400
From Mr J. H. Longmaid 15

DISBURSED.

Paid Helena Independent	$900
" C. D. Greenfield, compilation	165
" Jesse Wilson, stenographer	100
" O. C. Zoeckler, typewriter and mailing	80
" for postage, express and stationery ·	42
" Discount on county warrants	27
" Services secretary and treasurer	101
January 15 to June 30, 1892.	

$1,415

Yours truly,

B. BROWN, Sec. & Treas.

Following is the bill of the Independent Publishing Co., which
shows a discrepancy of $100 with the above, in the matter of pay-
ment to Wilson, stenographer:

HELENA, Mont., July 27, 1892.

IRRIGATION CONVENTION,

    To INDEPENDENT PUBLISHING CO.,

                —— DR. ——

April 23, Wilson, stenographic work	$100 00
" 2, 9,000 pamphlets	800 00
" 20, 500 note circulars	4 50
" 22, printing on 500 envelopes	1 75

                —— CR. ——

March 18, Cash	$200 00
" 26, "	100 00
April 4, Cash	100 00
" 20, "	100 00
" 23, "	100 00
June 6, "	100 00
" 22, "	100 00
" 27, "	100 00
July 11, "	6 25

$906 25 $906 25

RULES, REGULATIONS AND LIST OF CHARTER MEMBERS OF THE MONTANA STATE IRRIGATION SOCIETY.

[Instituted February 10, 1892.]

NAME, OBJECTS, ETC.

Sec. 1. The name of this association shall be "The Montana State Irrigation Society."

Sec. 2. The objects of the society are to promote among its members the arts and sciences connected with the economical use and application of water for the purpose of irrigation; the welfare of those employed in the different branches of irrigation; to recommend the enactment of suitable laws; the furtherance of research and experimentation with the different problems of irrigation as found in the state of Montana, these objects to be accomplished by means of meetings for social intercourse and the reading and discussion of papers; and to circulate by means of publications among its members the information thus obtained.

Sec. 3. The members of this society shall be persons interested in irrigation. To become a member of this society all persons must be proposed by a member, accompanied with a fee of admission and the applicant's postoffice address, and his application shall be referred to the committee on membership, consisting of three members of the executive committee, the secretary and the treasurer of the society, who shall examine his application, and if they deem the applicant a proper person, the secretary shall notify him and place his name upon the list of members. All persons admitted as members shall bind themselves to the observance of all by-laws, resolutions and regulations of the society that are now in force or may hereafter be adopted, under a penalty of forfeiture of membership. All memberships must be personal.

Sec. 4. The dues of members shall be $5, payable on their election, and $5 per annum thereafter, payable in advance at the annual meeting. Honorary members shall not be liable to dues. Any member in arrears may at the discretion of the executive committee be deprived of the receipt of publications or stricken from the list of members when in arrears for one year; provided, that he may be restored to membership by the executive committee on payment of all arrears or by re-election after an interval of two years.

OFFICERS.

Sec. 5. The officers of this society shall consist of a president, two vice presidents, a secretary, a treasurer and an executive committee. The executive committee shall consist of one member from each county, and five members of the executive committee shall constitute a quorum. The officers shall all be elected at the regular annual meeting, and shall hold their offices one year, or until their successors are elected and appointed. The duties of all the above officers shall be such as usually pertain to their offices or may be delegated to them by the executive committee or the society. The society shall also elect a commission of five engineers, who shall report at the annual meetings or if called upon by the executive committee, regarding the state of the science of irrigation. The president shall appoint one representative from each county in the state, whose duty it shall be to present at the annual meetings of the society a written report regarding the condition of the irrigation canals and ditches in his county. Such representatives shall be superintendents of canals or men actively engaged in the work of irrigation.

AMENDMENTS.

Sec. 6. These rules may be amended at any annual meeting by a two-thirds vote of the members present.

TIME AND PLACE OF MEETINGS.

Sec. 7. The annual meeting of this society shall be held on the second Thursday in January of each year. The place of holding such annual meetings shall be determined by vote of the society at its preceding annual meeting. The time and place of the quarterly meetings shall be fixed by the executive committee.

LIST OF OFFICERS.

JOHN M. ROBINSON, President, Bozeman.
I. D. O'DONNELL, First Vice President, Billings.
CHAS H WRIGHT, Second Vice President, Great Falls.
H. M. PARCHEN, Treasurer, Helena.
S. B. ROBBINS, Secretary, Great Falls.

EXECUTIVE COMMITTEE.

Beaverhead, W. M. Oliver; Cascade, H. P. Rolfe; Choteau, T. C. Burns; Custer, —— ——; Dawson, —— ——; Deer Lodge, ——; Flathead, Fred Whiteside; Fergus, ——; Gallatin, W. W. Alderson; Granite, —— ——; Jefferson, J. E. Keating; Lewis and Clarke, Donald Bradford; Meagher, W. H. Sutherlin; Missoula, ——; Madison, J. T Conner; Park, Alfred Meyers; Ravalli, ——; Silver Bow, —— ——; Teton, Z. T. Burton; Valley, —— ——; Yellowstone, ——.

COMMITTEE ON MEMBERSHIP.

H. M. Parchen, S. B. Robbins, H. P. Rolfe, W. W. Alderson and W. H. Sutherlin.

ENGINEERS COMMISSION.

John W. Wade, Chairman, Helena; S. B. Robbins, Great Falls; C. M. Thorpe, Bozeman.

CHARTER MEMBERS.

Alderson, W. W., Bozeman; Bradford, Donald, Helena, Browne, Jos. A., Melrose; Burns, T. C., Chinook; Burton, Z. T., Choteau; Conner, John T., Virginia City; Conrow, J. M., Livingston; Gilbert, Wm. R., Dillon; Harris, Lyman C., Box 974, Helena; Holter, A. M., Helena; Hoppe, H. J., Livingston; Keating, John A., Helena; McDonald, T. P., Red Lodge; Meyers, Alfred, Livingston; Murray, W. H., Belgrade; Nelson, A. H., Helena; O'Donnell, I. D., Billings; Oliver, W. M., Dillon; Parchen, H. M., Helena; Parker, W. F., Great Falls; Perkins, J. L., Helena; Porter, N. T., Great Falls; Quaintance, A. C., Boulder; Reese, Thomas, Bozeman; Rolfe, H. P., Great Falls; Robinson, John M., Bozeman; Robbins, S. B., Great Falls; Ryan, Ed., Finn; Sales, Chas., Salesville; Sanders, W. F., Helena; Shuart, B. F., Bozeman; Sutherlin, W. H., White Sulphur Springs; Swallow, G. C., Helena; Thorpe, C. M., Bozeman; Wade, John W., Helena; Winne, Peter, Helena; Whiteside, Fred, Kalispel; Wright, Chas. H., Great Falls.

.